Praise for

THE NO BULLSH*T GUIDE TO BUILDING BOOKS THAT GET READ

I've written two books using the *Brick by Brick* system. Both books were written quickly while still maintaining momentum with an organic feel. There will be times when you feel like you're getting off track, but trust the process. Not only did the result surpass my expectations, but I'm selling far more copies than I could have imagined.

— **Dr. Roland Cochrun, author of** *The High Achievers' Guide to Sex Addiction Recovery*

I was drowning in perfectionism until Ann told me, "Too polished. Shittier." It worked. My book exists because she knows how to get writers out of their own way. *Brick by Brick* is the straight-talking, bullshit-free roadmap every overthinking writer needs. As someone who coaches people through change for a living, I can tell you: Ann's method works. She's the rare combination of writing genius and pragmatic strategist. *Brick by Brick* doesn't just teach you how to write — it gives you permission to *finish*.

— **Oonagh Duncan, author of** *Healthy as F*ck*

Finally, a book about writing books that doesn't make you want to give up before you start. *Brick by Brick* understands that the biggest obstacle to writing isn't a lack of talent—it's feeling overwhelmed by the enormity of the task. The *Brick by Brick* method transforms paralyzing projects into achievable goals.
— John Beede, author of *Climb On!: Success Strategies for Teens*

The time is now to unleash your inner author with this proven, no-nonsense plan. *Brick by Brick* has zero patience for flashy writing advice that wastes your precious energy and momentum. Its sage, direct, and delightfully irreverent guidance cuts straight to what matters: getting your book written, revised, and into readers' hands. Your business – and the world – is waiting!
— Dr. Bridget Cooper, author of *Unflappable*

For recovering perfectionists who've been paralyzed by the idea of writing a "perfect" book, *Brick by Brick* offers the antidote. Ann provides a systematic approach that embraces the messy reality of creation while still producing a great outcome! Her way of helping you get past the "it's got to be perfect" mindset and the associated angst to achieve an outcome that *is* perfect is just brilliant. This book meets you where you are and then gracefully guides you to feeling good about what you're doing, brick by brick, piece by piece.
—Vicki Suiter, author of *The Profit Bleed*

In *Brick by Brick*, Ann Sheybani shows how to plan, test, and build your book the same way you'd build a business—intentionally and efficiently. It's a masterclass in thinking as both a writer and a strategist. Ann knows how to make books that aren't just coffee table decorations, but a workhorse that gets read, creates instant credibility, opens doors, and grows your business.

—Cecilia Hilkey, International Bestselling author of *The Perfectly Imperfect Family*

Brick by Brick is a "cut to the chase" book offering straightforward, occasionally cheeky advice on completing, polishing, and publishing your book. If you're tired of research paralysis and ready for real action, this is your book.

—Jules Wyman, author of *If We Can, You Can*

Brick by Brick is what I needed before I wasted six months pretending my "book process" was anything more than sophisticated procrastination. Ann doesn't hand you inspirational fairy dust; she gives you a system for people who are done researching and ready to actually finish the damn thing. The brick-by-brick method isn't cute; it's construction. If you're tired of writing advice that makes you feel motivated for 48 hours and accomplished for zero, this is how you build something real.

—Kristen Arnold, Founder, Business Builders United and International Bestselling author of *The Wisdom Collective*

Brick by Brick is like having Ann Sheybani walking right beside you on your writing journey, looking over your shoulder and whispering in your ear. She knows the way—the pitfalls, the rabbit holes, the sidetracks, and the shortcuts. She has the map, the compass, and an understanding of the terrain because she's been there. You couldn't ask for a better companion. Whatever the genre, *Brick by Brick* is an expert guide that will cut through the noise and lead you to a finished product.

—Dr. Thomas Garcia, author of *The Difference*

Brick by Brick cuts through the industry noise with a refreshingly practical approach to book writing. Instead of vague inspiration, it provides concrete steps that turn overwhelming book projects into manageable daily tasks. This isn't just another 'follow your dreams' writing guide—it's a strategic blueprint that actually works. And it's the formula behind my #1 international best-selling book.

—May Busch, #1 International Bestselling author of *Visible brick by brick*

THE NO BULLSH*T GUIDE TO BUILDING BOOKS THAT GET READ

Ann Sheybani

SUMMIT PRESS
Publisher

Printed in the United States of America
First Printing, 2025
ISBN: 979-8-9852063-9-5

Summit Press Publishers
P.O. Box 1356
Intervale, New Hampshire 03845

For information about working with Ann Sheybani, visit www.summitpresspublishers.com

For bulk sales, email us at author@summitpresspublishers.com.

TABLE OF CONTENTS

STEP 2

Creating A Shitty First Draft

STEP 3

Developing An Outline

INTRODUCTION

Know how to eat an elephant? Yes, that's right: one small bite at a time. That's how you write a book, run a marathon, earn a college degree—how you accomplish any hairy, audacious goal worthy of your time and energy. You know that; everybody does. You know better than to contemplate massive goals in their entirety. You know that, to avoid paralysis and/or nervous breakdowns, you need to chunk the thing down into manageable pieces—bricks that you can handle one at a time. After all, that's why you're holding this no-bullshit guide in your hands. A goal without a plan is just a wish. And you're done wishing.

Welcome. Welcome to that moment. You're about to take that first bite of elephant. You're about to turn your clever ideas into a real, live book. You're done talking about it; you just are. You've grown bored (along with everybody else) with all those highly imaginative excuses you've concocted for not sitting down to write. The grout bleaching will just have to wait, as will the closet rearranging, and the unicorn grooming. You're ready, finally, to turn those cocktail napkin musings into something tangible. Plan in hand, you're ready to take action. You're going to start right here, right now. We—you and I—are going to get this party started.

Before we dive deeper, let me address something that might be bugging you already. Yes, I know mixing metaphors is supposedly a cardinal sin of writing. Nobody likes it when authors start with elephants and suddenly pivot to brick construction like some confused urban planner. But let's stop and examine my reasoning for breaking this sacred writing rule.

The original title of this book was *How to Eat the Elephant: Build Your Book in Bite-Sized Steps.* Charming, right? Except for one tiny problem: absolutely no one searches Amazon using the keywords "bite-sized" or "eat-the-elephant" when they're looking for help with their book projects. Trust me, I learned this the hard way. (Although, come to think of it, bricklayers are going to be mighty disappointed to discover that they're on their own with that barbecue pit they're trying to construct.)

Here's how the metaphors work together and why I'm keeping both: Eating an elephant represents the overall mindset—tackling any overwhelming project one manageable piece at a time. Building with bricks represents the specific method— creating individual content pieces you'll eventually assemble into your finished book. Both metaphors support the same philosophy: breaking complex projects into manageable steps that lead to real results, not utter paralysis.

Why This Revision Exists

Before diving deeper, let me explain why you're holding a revised version of a book I wrote in 2014. The short answer? Everything changed. The writing landscape, the publishing industry, the tools available to writers, the competition for readers' attention—it all shifted dramatically. What worked in

2014 doesn't necessarily work in 2025, and I'd be doing you a disservice pretending otherwise.

But more importantly, I changed. And that evolution taught me things about writing and publishing that I wish I'd known when I first put this guide together, kinda like that title thing.

My Expert Positioning Story (or: How I Learned to Stop Worrying and Love Strategy)

Picture this: A 38-year-old woman walks into Harvard armed with a compelling story about living in Iran with her traditionally conservative husband and dreams of becoming the next big literary name. That was me in the early 2000s, convinced that good writing plus an MFA would equal publishing success. Oh, how adorably naive I was. Cute, even.

I had early success with short stories and personal essays, making the whole writing appear seductively simple. I thought I could toss some ideas on the page, juggle a few words, sharpen some verbs, and win a Pushcart Prize before sunset. Five memoir drafts later, reality delivered its first cold slap.

The second slap came at a prestigious writing conference where I pitched my memoir to agents and publishers. Without a platform, compelling synopsis, or marketing plan demonstrating market viability, it became crystal clear that my beautifully crafted manuscript wouldn't be purchased, published, or promoted by any big New York house. Mind you, this was before the traditional publishing industry imploded, and all those disinterested gatekeepers lost their jobs. Not that I'm gloating or anything.

So, I did what any sensible writer does when faced with rejection: I started a blog and founded East Hill Writers' Workshop with a couple of talented partners. We focused on craft—teaching novelists, memoirists, children's book writers, and short story writers to build bodies of work over years-long timelines. Pure literary pursuit. Noble stuff.

Then, my husband's Tony Robbins coaching colleagues asked me to teach their clients how to write books. These weren't aspiring literary darlings; these were successful entrepreneurs and professionals who wanted to write books for all sorts of reasons—some familiar to me from my literary background, others completely foreign. These nice people had six-week timelines, not six-year ones, another mic-drop as far as I was concerned.

I was fascinated by the concept of wanting a book that would build your business, establish your expertise, or launch a speaking career. Soon I was inundated with requests to help people write expert-positioning books. That evolved from content development to book doctoring to ghostwriting. I wrote book proposals for those wanting traditional publishing deals. When traditional publishers turned some of them down, I figured out the entire publishing game and eventually opened my own hybrid press.

Because we specialized in helping experts and thought leaders, strategy became everything. We weren't just creating books but serving readers while simultaneously serving authors' career goals. We built platforms, launched courses, created social media content, and developed speeches. We became a one-stop shop for authors who understood that a book could be the cornerstone of something much bigger.

This journey taught me that the divide between "literary" writers and "commercial" writers is artificial nonsense. Strong craft and strategic thinking serve all writers, regardless of their motivations. The Beautiful Writer crafting literary fiction benefits from understanding the audience and market just as much as the Expert Positioner building a business around their expertise.

What's Different in 2025

The publishing landscape I navigated all those years ago looks quaint compared to today's reality. Back then, you competed primarily against other books. Now, you're competing against TikTok videos, YouTube tutorials, podcasts, newsletters, and an ocean of free content that promises instant answers to every question.

But here's the flip side: The tools available to writers in 2025 would have seemed magical ten years ago. AI can help with research and initial drafts (though it can't replace your authentic voice—more on that later). Online platforms now connect you directly with beta readers. Social media lets you test content and build audiences while you write. Publishing options exist for every budget and timeline.

The bad news? It's harder to break through the noise.

The good news? If you combine strong writing with strategic thinking, you have more paths to success than ever before.

And here's something I wish I'd understood earlier: you can build your platform while you write your book. In fact, the more you do this—testing content, engaging with your future audience, establishing your expertise—the better your book's chances of success.

What You Can Expect

Let me give you an overview of what we'll cover in this revised edition.

I'd like to begin by introducing you to some simple, get-your-rump-in-that-seat tools that will keep you writing, even when Netflix whispers seductively from the next room.

Then, before we explore the different types of books (genres) you might want to write and the time and skill required for many of them, we're going to focus on the Why. Why, pray tell, do you want to write this book? The Why always comes before the What (genre). Knowing your Why will allow you to make informed decisions about everything from timeline to publishing method to marketing strategy.

We'll talk about the writing process—what it looks like to take a project from concept to publication in the current era, as opposed to that fantasy you developed watching *Finding Forrester*. This may also be a good place to mention the timeframe required for completing a book. Contrary to what some internet marketers would have you believe, writing a book worth reading will likely take longer than 48 hours. (Though with modern tools and the right strategy, it doesn't have to take years either.)

Once the dust settles, we'll begin gathering content for your book. We'll create new material and identify stuff you may already have lying around—blog posts, articles, presentations, and social media content. There's nothing more satisfying than repurposing material you've already invested time in creating.

Of course, once we've got plenty of material to work with (I like to think of it as clay), it's time to begin forming bricks. Here's where the magic happens: instead of trying to write an entire book from start to finish—which paralyzes most people before they type the first sentence—you'll write one brick at a time. Bricks are individual content pieces: stories, frameworks, case studies, research—whatever your genre requires. Each brick is manageable, completable, and serves as a building block you'll later arrange into a cohesive book structure.

This brick-by-brick approach breaks the overwhelming task of "writing a book" into doable daily work. You're not staring at a blank document wondering how to fill 200 pages; you're crafting one compelling story, developing one useful framework, or researching one case study.

But here's the strategic advantage that modern writers have: you can test these bricks with your target audience as you create them. Share that story in a newsletter, present that framework at a conference, post that case study on LinkedIn. You'll discover which content resonates, which needs refinement, and which ideas you should abandon before investing months in a full manuscript. This isn't just about building an audience—though that happens—it's about ensuring your book delivers real value to the people you're trying to reach.

Throughout this process, you'll have access to proven templates and frameworks that take the guesswork out of structuring your book. I've included downloadable templates for the most popular nonfiction genres, plus guides for creating compelling titles and other essential resources that will save you months of trial and error. You can find them at www.summitpresspublishers.com/brick.

A huge pile of bricks is great, you say, but what am I supposed to do with them all? How will they fit together? No worries, because we're going to develop an architectural blueprint for your book. This outline—because that's what this architectural blueprint is—will show you where to place these separate bricks, so you create cohesion. We're also going to give your book a working title that will make it feel alarmingly real, keeping you motivated.

Throughout this entire process, I'll show you how to build your platform for your book in a way that supports rather than detracts from your ultimate goal of completing your manuscript. You'll learn to leverage your book-writing journey to establish expertise, connect with readers, and create anticipation for your finished work—without falling into the endless content creation trap that derails so many authors.

Did I mention the trouble you'll run into along the way? There will be barricades, barbed wire, and open manhole covers. We'll discuss tenacity, doubt, boredom, and being okay with your shitty first draft. We'll talk about where to find continuing support, how to identify fixes from other books during revision, and how to navigate that seemingly never-ending, lonely path ahead.

For those preferring to see their musings in print sooner rather than later, we'll explore hiring professionals to clean up your draft—where to find these angels of mercy and what their services cost in 2025. (Spoiler alert: none of this is cheap.)

Before we wrap up, we're having a little church chat about the publishing industry. I'll explain the differences between traditional, hybrid, and self-publishing in today's market. We'll discuss advances, agents, query letters, platforms, promotion, and AI tools. We're talking about these things because understanding your options will keep you motivated during the writing process. Even without an MFA or massive social media following, you'll have viable paths to publication.

This Strategic Writing Partner of Yours

Listen, I know all your excuses for not settling down to write your book because I've used them myself. Hell, I invented them. I know exactly how to start a novel and then abandon it on page 84. I know exactly how to complete the fourth draft of a memoir and then file it away indefinitely. I can't count the number of nonfiction projects I've started and left to rot. I know how to write, rewrite, and rewrite some more, then give up because the process feels impossible. I know about doubt, fear, procrastination, and perfectionism. In other words, I see you, and I've been there. I'm wearing the T-shirt right now.

But I also know something else now: I know what it looks like when accomplished professionals combine their expertise with strategic writing and complete books that serve both readers and their business goals. I've seen Beautiful Writers discover that understanding their audience enhances rather than compromises their art. I've watched Expert Positioners realize that compelling storytelling makes their insights one thousand times more powerful. I've guided Practical Professionals through creating books that advance their careers while genuinely helping readers. (If you're wondering which type of writer you are, don't you worry; we'll get to that.)

Since starting my practice as a content strategist in 2007, I've worked with hundreds of writers across every genre and motivation. Some want literary recognition, others want business growth, and many want both. What I've learned is this: regardless of why you're writing, success comes from combining strong craft with strategic thinking.

My role is to serve as your thought and accountability partner, helping you to cut through the bullshit and navigate from concept to published book while maintaining the quality and integrity that matter to you. It doesn't matter if your timeline is six weeks, six months, or six years—your mission is completing that first draft, so you'll have the one thing separating you from dreamers: something tangible to work with.

So, yeah, I know. I know each obstacle and excuse for not writing a book because I've navigated those rapids myself. But more importantly, I know how to help you work through them strategically.

Ready to begin? Let's dive into Chapter 1 and set you up for success. Turn the page. And remember—we're going to work smart, not hard. This process can actually be enjoyable when you have the right strategy.

STEP 1

ON YOUR MARK, GET SET, GO

1

PREPARING FOR GREATNESS

Building Writing Habits That Actually Work

I t's time to prepare for greatness. How does one do that, you ask?

First things first: Writers need structure. This was a hard lesson for me to learn because I hate structure. See, I like to be freewheeling. I dig going with the flow, the wind streaming through my hair, and seeing where the road takes me. "Don't fence me in" is my favorite motto. But this philosophy causes me problems as a writer. For a writer, freedom can be our worst enemy. It can lead to paralysis, procrastination, aimlessness, and indecision.

To make matters worse, you're not just writing a book anymore. You're building a platform, establishing a readership for your book, maybe your expertise, and creating content that will serve your professional goals for years, regardless of what they are. This makes structure even more critical because you're juggling multiple moving parts—your writing, audience development, and content testing. Tell me that doesn't make you want to kick yourself free of any and all constraints.

The problem with creating structure for us whimsical types is that it doesn't just happen on its own because we hope it will. We have to develop some very particular practices and commit to them. We can't just give them lip service.

So, it's time to get organized and prioritize writing. You can still be freewheeling in other areas of your life. Go ahead and eat oatmeal for dinner, wear white after Labor Day, or change your name to Ted. Just pick some other way to rail against the man.

Set Some Actual Goals

It's also time to set some SMART goals. If you've never encountered the acronym SMART, it stands for specific, measurable, actionable, realistic, and time-defined. Here's an example of a SMART goal: I will write at least twenty pages of my book by Friday evening of this week. It's specific—those twenty pages; actionable—unless your hands get cut off in a horrible lawnmower accident; realistic—unless you legitimately can't write or type; and time-defined—what with you finishing up by Friday night.

Here's an example of a stupid goal: I really should get to my book this week if I can break away from The Shopping Network. You see the difference? Thought so.

But here's the modern twist: your SMART goals should include platform development alongside your writing. For example: "I will write one chapter this week and test the key concept from that chapter in a LinkedIn post to see how my audience responds." This dual approach ensures you're not writing in isolation, as authors did in previous years.

By the way, you'll hear me talk about LinkedIn as if it were the only social media site worth frequenting, but if you're a regular on Facebook or Snapchat or whatever, feel free to superimpose. That said, if you're a professional looking to write a book to establish your authority, how can you not be on LinkedIn? Hello! Time to wake up.

Three Things You Need to Do

To develop that necessary structure (I'm talking to you, oh resistant, rebellious types), we're going to do three things:

1. Take Out Your Calendar.

It doesn't matter if your calendar is the old-fashioned paper variety or the online type. (Personally, I love Google Calendar, especially its nagging alarm reminders.) We're going to begin by setting some writing appointments for the week—some SMART appointments.

Because the mind works best when you can focus, uninterrupted, on a task for a reasonable amount of time—not too little, and not too long, something just right for you and your untreated ADHD—we'll create some blocks. It may take a session or two to get a feel for which time block works best for you, but for now, choose between the following:

- Two 3-hour writing sessions per week or
- Three 2-hour writing sessions per week.

Now, pen these into your calendar in blood. Will you write from 8:00 to 10:00 a.m. on Monday, Wednesday, and Friday? Or will you write from 9:00 p.m. to midnight on Saturday and Sunday? Choose. You know best what will work with your hectic schedule and what time of day your brain functions optimally. You can reasonably predict when the kids, the dog, or your partner will be otherwise occupied.

By the way, this is a great time to draw some healthy boundaries around you and your dreams and to teach your loved ones that there are certain times when you'll be unavailable—unless, of course, someone has broken their leg.

I happen to be a morning person. I'm at my best before noon. I like to write three times a week, just after I go for my morning run. That's when ideas tend to flow for me; that's when I have time and space to think, when I'm least likely to be interrupted.

But you may be a night owl. You might prefer to sit down at midnight and lose yourself to the sound of the ticking clock. Maybe you stay focused for three hours at a time because that's how you roll. Maybe two hours work best for you because you get tired and want to hit the hay.

You know yourself. Follow your own rhythms. What works for other people may not work for you.

Regardless, six hours a week is a manageable and realistic goal. You don't have to quit your day job to fit your writing time in, nor do you have to give up your friends and family, even if you'd sometimes like to.

Now, you're also going to want to schedule 30 minutes after each writing session for platform development. This might mean turning your writing session insights into a LinkedIn post, adding to your newsletter draft, or updating your other social media sites with progress. The key is making platform building part of your routine, not an afterthought. (Don't hate the messenger.)

Be forewarned: without regular writing appointments, you will wander off, dragging out the process of writing a book for years on end. Without platform building, you might as well release your book to outer space because no one will read it.

2. Get a Notebook For Your Story Ideas.

When you write consistently, ideas will begin to come to you when you least expect them. The unconscious mind becomes your little unpaid helper. Buy a notebook, any kind you like, and carry it everywhere you go, even out to dinner or church. Someone clever or really dumb will say something to spark your imagination, and, man, you'll want to capture that. Or suddenly, that line of dialogue, that aspect of character, or that supporting argument you've been struggling with will magically appear. Fail to write it down, and it will evaporate into thin air.

If you feel uncomfortable scribbling in the presence of others, particularly among those who sigh a lot, excuse yourself and run to the nearest restroom. Whatever it takes, get the good stuff down before it's lost to the ether.

When you read other books and get a flash of inspiration, jot those ideas down in your story notebook as well.

Your phone can also serve this purpose through voice memos or note apps, though something about physical writing helps ideas stick. Use whatever method ensures you actually capture the thoughts instead of losing them.

Now, here's where the regular practice comes in. Right before bed or first thing in the morning, make some notes in your story notebook. Do this every day, even if you've captured something fabulous while out and about. I promise it will become a habit you'll not want to give up, like brushing your teeth. (At least I hope you don't want to give up on brushing your teeth.)

The notes you jot down can include questions: How am I going to weave in the backstory of my protagonist's first marriage? Or random ideas: Write about the streets of Abadan in as much detail as possible. Or thoughts about structure: *Maybe I should switch up the narrator in alternating chapters—first Doris, then Bufford. Did I capture that brilliant tip in the bullet point list in Chapter 10?*

Because we're all about platform integration, also note potential content ideas: *This client transformation story could work as a case study in Chapter 5 and as a LinkedIn post.* You're training yourself to think like a content creator, not just a writer.

We're going to come back to the story notebook when we discuss creating content. Right now, you're digging a well from which to draw.

3. Get a Separate Notebook For Your Morning Pages.

Morning Pages is a tool developed by Julia Cameron in *The Artist's Way* to clear your mind for the day. If you haven't read her book, you should.

Here's how it works: Before your day gets busy, before you shower or fiddle with breakfast, sit with a devoted notebook and write down three pages of random thoughts. Stream of consciousness. Write whatever comes to mind: a note to pick up the dry cleaning, some thoughts on that fool at the office who stole your stapler, a description of the hors d'oeuvres you want to serve at your dinner party.

Get the garbage swirling around in your head onto the page. Forget about editing or worrying about grammar or spelling; let your pen move rapidly across the page from start to finish. By doing this, you open your creative channels to better focus on your project and experience a valuable writing mode, free of the impulse to edit. We'll talk about the dangers of "editing in the field" before the proverbial sun has set.

The Platform-Building Mindset

Newsflash: today's successful authors don't write their books in isolation and then hope to find an audience. They build their audience while writing, using the book content to fuel their platform development. (You're going to hear me repeat this concept like a broken record.)

This doesn't mean compromising your creative vision or pandering to social media algorithms. It means being strategic about sharing your expertise and insights as you develop them.

Big-name authors like Mel Robbins, Brené Brown, and Tim Ferriss built their platforms while developing their book content. They tested ideas through articles, speeches, and social media before committing them to book form. By launch day, they had engaged audiences eagerly waiting for the complete framework.

P.S. If you're writing a memoir or fiction, your favorite authors shared their process in real time or paid someone to do that. Take a look at J.K. Rowling, Margaret Atwood, and Elizabeth Gilbert, and you'll see how actively engaged they are with their audiences while they're working on their books.

You can do the same thing. Use your writing time to create book content, then use your platform development time to test and share key insights with your audience.

What You're Really Signing Up For

Let's be clear about what preparing for greatness requires: a commitment to doing work that most people are too lazy or scared to attempt.

You'll write when you don't feel like writing. You'll share your work before it feels ready. You'll engage with your audience consistently, not just when you remember to. You'll revise ruthlessly because great books are rewritten, not written.

This isn't about becoming a social media influencer or sacrificing your artistic integrity. It's about being professional and strategic with your work, so it actually reaches the people who need it.

Why Structure Matters More Than Ever

Without structure, you'll end up like 99 % of aspiring authors, with a half-finished manuscript gathering digital dust while you wonder why writing feels so hard. Soooooo harrrdddd.

With structure, you'll join the small percentage of people who finish their books, build their platforms, and achieve their professional goals through writing.

The choice is yours. But choose before you start writing, because developing these habits after you're stuck is much harder than building them from the beginning. Ask me how I know.

The structure you build now will determine whether you're still talking about writing your book five years from now or leveraging the professional credibility that comes from being a published author.

DO THIS

1. Take out your calendar. Commit to and schedule two three-hour sessions or three two-hour sessions this week. You'll be doing this each week for the foreseeable future. Nurture the habit. Don't make me repeat myself.

2. Buy two notebooks—one for your stories and one for your morning pages. If you're more digital, set up equivalent systems on your phone or computer.

3. Each morning, write three Morning Pages to flush your mental toilet.

4. Make a few notes in your story notebook each evening to keep your project percolating.

5. Schedule 30 minutes after each writing session for platform development—testing ideas, engaging with your audience, or creating supporting content.

6. Stop making excuses about not having time or perfect conditions. Professional writers create the necessary conditions instead of waiting for them to appear magically.

2

WHY, WHY, WHY, WHY, WHY

Identify Your Writer Type and Stop Wasting Time

Can I ask you a question? Why do you want to write a book? Seriously, do you even know? What's your purpose for doing so?

After working with hundreds of writers over the past decade, I've learned that there are fundamentally different types of people who want to write books, and they have completely different motivations. Understanding which type you are isn't just helpful—it's essential for choosing the right genre, developing the right strategy, and avoiding years of frustration.

When I first started working with writers way back when, most of my clients fell into what I'll call the Beautiful Writer category. They wanted to create art, tell compelling stories, craft elegant prose, and be recognized for their literary talent. Their dream was to see their book in bookstores, get positive reviews, and maybe win awards.

However, as my career evolved and the publishing landscape shifted dramatically, I began working with a completely different type of writer. These people weren't primarily motivated by artistic recognition or beautiful prose. They wanted to be seen as experts. They wanted to build audiences interested in their content. They wanted to develop careers and businesses that didn't require selling 20,000 or more books a month to survive.

They dreamed of being on stage, being interviewed, becoming the next Brené Brown, or building influence in their industries. The book wasn't the end goal for these writers—it was a strategic tool for achieving much larger professional ambitions.

All approaches are valid. But they require entirely different strategies, and most writing advice ignores this distinction.

Now, let me break down the different types of writers I work with so you can figure out where you fit.

The Beautiful Writer

Core Motivation: To create art, craft compelling narratives, and be recognized for literary talent

Primary Goals:

1. Write novels, memoirs, or literary nonfiction that moves readers deeply
2. Develop a distinctive voice and style

3. Get published by traditional publishers
4. Receive critical acclaim and positive reviews
5. Build a readership that appreciates quality writing
6. Leave a literary legacy

Success Metrics:

1. Book sales and readership
2. Critical reviews and literary awards
3. Recognition from the writing community
4. Personal satisfaction with the craft
5. Emotional impact on readers

Typical Genres: Literary fiction, memoir, creative nonfiction, poetry, short story collections

Platform Needs: Moderate. A website, some social media presence, and possibly a newsletter. Your platform should serve your book; you need enough online presence to connect with readers and support your book launches, but platform building isn't your primary focus.

Reality Check: This path requires exceptional writing skill, a thick skin for rejection, and often takes years to achieve recognition. Most Beautiful Writers need day jobs to support their writing unless they achieve significant commercial success.

If you're a Beautiful Writer, that's wonderful. The world needs people who prioritize craft, storytelling, and artistic expression. Just understand that your path differs from the others, and most of this book's platform-building advice may feel unnecessary or even offensive to your artistic sensibilities. But stand down for a hot minute. You might learn something useful.

The Expert Positioner

Core Motivation: To be recognized as a leading expert in their field and to build a business around their knowledge

Primary Goals:

1. Establish credibility and authority in their industry
2. Attract better clients and charge higher fees
3. Generate speaking opportunities and media coverage
4. Build an engaged audience interested in their expertise
5. Create multiple revenue streams from their knowledge
6. Become the go-to person when people need help in their area

Success Metrics:

1. Professional opportunities generated by the book
2. Speaking engagements and media appearances
3. Client quality and fees
4. Audience size and engagement
5. Revenue growth from expertise-based services
6. Industry recognition and influence

Typical Genres: Business books, self-help, how-to guides, expert positioning books, big idea books

Platform Needs: Extensive. Your book serves your platform, which means you need to build your audience while writing, test your concepts publicly, and use your book as one component of a larger business strategy.

Reality Check: Your book is one component of a larger business strategy. You need to think like an entrepreneur, not just a writer. If that sounds overwhelming, welcome to the modern publishing world.

The Influential Storyteller

Core Motivation: To share their life experiences in ways that inspire, teach, and influence others while building a personal brand

Primary Goals:

1. Tell their story in a way that helps others
2. Build a following around their life experiences and lessons learned
3. Generate speaking opportunities about resilience, transformation, or overcoming challenges
4. Position themselves as motivational speakers or life coaches
5. Create a movement or inspire social change
6. Become known for their unique perspective on universal challenges

Success Metrics:

1. Audience engagement and emotional response
2. Speaking opportunities and media coverage
3. Impact stories from readers who have applied their lessons

4. Social media following and influence
5. Revenue from speaking, coaching, or related services
6. Recognition as a thought leader in their area

Typical Genres: Memoirs, inspirational books (sometimes called motivational books), social justice narratives

Platform Needs: High. Your platform and your book grow together. Your personal story becomes your professional brand, and you must publicly share that journey while writing.

Reality Check: You need to be comfortable sharing your life publicly and consistently engaging with your audience. If you're not prepared for that level of transparency, pick a different path.

The Oprah Stage Dreamer

Core Motivation: To achieve widespread recognition, influence, and a platform that reaches millions of people

Primary Goals:

1. Write a book that becomes a cultural phenomenon
2. Appear on major media outlets and influential stages
3. Build a massive following across multiple platforms
4. Become a household name in their area of expertise
5. Generate significant revenue from books, speaking, and media appearances
6. Influence public conversations and social change

Success Metrics:

1. Bestseller list appearances
2. Major media coverage and interviews
3. Social media followers and engagement
4. Speaking fees and event bookings
5. Cultural impact and influence
6. Revenue from multiple streams

Typical Genres: Big idea books, memoirs with universal appeal, social commentary, transformational stories

Platform Needs: Massive and professionally managed. You're competing for attention with established celebrities and thought leaders. This requires significant investment in professional support.

Reality Check: This level of success requires exceptional content, strategic marketing, often significant financial investment, and frequently some element of luck or timing. Most people who achieve this level have been building their platforms for years before their book launches. If you start from scratch and expect to land on Oprah's stage within two years, you may be delusional.

The Practical Professional

Core Motivation: To enhance their current career and professional reputation without necessarily building a massive platform

Primary Goals:

1. Establish credibility in their current field
2. Attract better job opportunities or clients
3. Share their expertise in a structured way
4. Build a professional network and recognition
5. Create a legacy of their professional knowledge
6. Differentiate themselves from competitors

Success Metrics:

1. Professional opportunities and career advancement
2. Industry recognition and peer respect
3. Quality of new clients or job offers
4. Professional network growth
5. Personal satisfaction with sharing knowledge

Typical Genres: Industry-specific guides, business books, professional memoirs, how-to books

Platform Needs: Modest and industry-specific. Your book serves your existing career rather than creating a new one. A LinkedIn presence, professional associations, and industry events may be sufficient.

Reality Check: The ROI comes through professional advancement rather than book sales. Don't expect to quit your day job or become famous. Expect to become more credible in your current field.

Are there other types of writers? Yes, there's The Passionate Scholar, and The Creative Explorer, and The Journalist, and The....

My Philosophy: Craft + Strategy = Success

After working with all these different types of writers, I've learned that the most successful authors, regardless of their primary motivation, combine two essential elements: strong writing and strategic thinking.

Let me be clear: well-crafted writing underpins everything, regardless of what kind of writer you are. You can have the best platform-building strategy in the world, but if your writing is sloppy, unclear, or boring, your book won't serve anyone—not you, not your readers, not your professional goals.

Equally important is strategic thinking—considering the outcome for you, the writer, and the reader. Just expressing yourself for the sake of expressing yourself is a zero-sum game. If your book doesn't serve a purpose beyond making you feel good about having written something, you're wasting everyone's time, including your own.

The Beautiful Writers who succeed don't just craft elegant sentences—they think strategically about reader experience, emotional impact, and how to reach their intended audience. The Expert Positioners who build lasting careers don't just focus on business outcomes—they develop their craft so their writing is clear, compelling, and genuinely helpful.

This doesn't mean every book needs to be a practical how-to guide. A beautifully crafted novel serves readers by providing entertainment, emotional connection, and perhaps new perspectives on the human experience. A well-written memoir serves readers by helping them feel less alone in their struggles or inspired by someone else's journey.

But if your book exists solely for your own self-expression without consideration for reader value, you're essentially asking people to pay money to read your diary. That's not a sustainable approach to book writing, and frankly, it's a little grandiose.

Why Your "Why" Determines Everything

Your why for writing this book—and you have to be very honest with yourself—will help determine what type of book you write, what genre it falls into, how much platform building you need to do, and what success will look like.

There is no "right" motivation for writing a book; it's different for everybody. Be brutally honest with yourself. It's okay to want to be seen as an expert, not an artist. You can yearn to tell your life story, not teach a useful skill, without labeling yourself a first-class narcissist. You can dream of being on Oprah's stage without being delusional about the work required to get there.

Don't make life harder for yourself by ignoring your real motivation or pretending you're motivated by something more "noble" than you actually are. The truth is good. Self-deception is a waste of everyone's time.

The Beautiful Writer who pretends they don't care about recognition will struggle with marketing because they haven't prepared themselves mentally for the business side of publishing. The Expert Positioner who insists they're writing for artistic reasons will choose the wrong genre and waste years writing something that doesn't serve their professional goals. The Oprah Stage Dreamer who won't admit their ambitions will underinvest in platform building and wonder why their book doesn't break through.

Be honest about what you really want, then align your strategy accordingly.

Put Your Why to Work

Writing a book is a process that will consume months or years of your life. From time to time, you'll question yourself and the relevance of your words. Other people will offer suggestions or opinions that will stir up doubt. Go back to your "why." Use it as a touchstone to ground yourself.

But more importantly, use your "why" to make strategic decisions about genre, platform building, content development, and marketing. Your motivation should drive every major decision you make about your book.

The sooner you get clear about your real motivations, the sooner you can start making strategic decisions that serve your goals instead of some romanticized version of what you think writing should be about.

DO THIS

1. Choose your writer type. Be brutally honest about which category describes your true motivations, not which one sounds most noble or artistic.

2. Answer this question in sickening detail: I want to write this book for/because...

3. And this one: I want my readers to understand...

4. Define success for your book: What would need to happen for you to consider your book a success? Be specific about metrics that matter to your writer type.

5. Assess the gap: Based on your writer type, what do you need to develop besides writing skills? Platform building? Media training? Professional editing? Business strategy?

6. Commit to your path: Stop trying to be the kind of writer you think you should be and embrace the type of writer you actually are.

3

CHOOSING YOUR GENRE

Match Your Book Type to Your Writer Type

Armed with your "Why" from Chapter 2, it's time to decide on a genre for your book. But before you can make a reasonable decision—one you're not going to constantly waffle back and forth on—we need to stop wandering the literary aisles like confused shoppers and start thinking strategically.

Most writers approach genre selection like they're at a bookstore buffet, sampling everything that looks appetizing. That's backwards and exhausting. Your genre should serve your goals, not your ego or your romantic notions about what type of writer you want to be.

I've watched way too many brilliant professionals waste months agonizing over whether to write a novel or a business book, as if the universe cares about their artistic angst. Meanwhile, their expertise sits unused, and their audience remains underserved.

Knock it off, I want to scream.

Let me give you a strategic framework for making this decision quickly and correctly, so you don't do the same.

A Quick Note on Prescriptive Nonfiction

Oh, hold on a sec. Before we dive into the decision-making questions, let me clarify a term you'll hear me use throughout this book: prescriptive nonfiction. This is an umbrella term that covers any book that teaches readers how to do something, solve a problem, or improve their lives.

Prescriptive nonfiction includes business books, self-help guides, how-to books, expert positioning books, big idea books, inspirational books, and workbooks. What these genres share is a focus on helping readers achieve specific outcomes. Unlike memoir or fiction, which primarily entertain or inspire, prescriptive nonfiction promises readers they'll learn something useful they can apply to their lives or work.

Why does this distinction matter? Because prescriptive nonfiction requires a different approach to writing, revision, and platform building than narrative genres. You're not just telling a story—you're solving problems and delivering results. That changes everything about how you develop and test your content.

Okay, let's proceed.

The Strategic Decision-Making Questions

Instead of wandering through a literary catalog or rehashing your motivations from Chapter 2, answer these four questions to pinpoint your genre:

1. What's Your Skill and Timeline Reality?

- **High writing experience + years to invest**
  If this is how you'd describe yourself, go with memoir, literary fiction, comprehensive big idea books, or original research books.
- **Moderate writing experience + months to invest**
  Consider how-to guides, business books, expert positioning books, or inspirational books.
- **Limited writing experience + want results quickly**
  You may want to stick to quote collections, simple how-to guides, workbooks, or interview-based books.
- **Weekend warriors with existing content**
  Anthologies, content compilations, or photo books with captions are your best bets.

Here's the unpleasant sitch, which I'll serve with a side of compassion, because that's how I roll: If you haven't taken a writing class since 1974 and want to write the next great American novel, you're setting yourself up for years of frustration and a very expensive therapy bill. Match your ambitions to your current skill level and available time.

And before you get your hackles up, let me point out that simple doesn't mean worthless. *Grumpy Cat*—written by a brother and sister team who made more money than God— was once listed at number 10 on the Motivational and How-to Bestseller List. If you want proof that simple concepts can become massive successes, find *Grumpy Cat* on Amazon and look inside. You don't have to write *The Grapes of Wrath* to have financial and literary success on your hands.

2. Do You Need Fiction or Nonfiction?

Choose nonfiction if:

- You want to establish expertise or credibility.
- You have real-world examples and case studies.
- Your goal is professional advancement.
- You want to teach, inspire, or guide readers.

Choose fiction if:

- You want artistic recognition.
- Your story is better served through imagination.
- You can handle longer timelines and more complex craft requirements.
- You're comfortable with uncertain commercial prospects.

For most business professionals and experts, fiction is a scenic detour from your real goals. Unless you're secretly harboring literary genius, be real about what you're trying to accomplish and pick the path that gets you there.

If you're still hemming and hawing, however, here's a practical way to test this decision: Take a pivotal moment from your life and write it both ways. Let's say your mother made you deliver Avon orders on your bike when you were a kid, and the neighborhood boys taunted you mercilessly. That experience taught you something important about resilience, entrepreneurship, or standing up for yourself.

Write it as nonfiction first—exactly what happened, how humiliated you felt pedaling through the neighborhood with that white basket full of lipstick and face cream, what you learned from the experience, and how readers can apply that lesson to overcome their own challenges.

Then write it as fiction—maybe you're still delivering something on your bike, but this time you ride off into the sunset to join the circus, or the neighborhood bullies get their comeuppance in creative ways that real life never provided, or you discover the lipstick has unearthly powers.

Which version serves your goals better? Which one feels more compelling to write and gets you excited about the possibilities? That's your answer.

3. What If I Want to Write a Book This Weekend?

Let me address the elephant in the room: all those programs promising you can write a book in 48 hours. Can you actually do this? The answer is yes and hell no, depending on what you mean by "write a book."

The answer is yes if:

- You have loads of existing content (blog posts, presentations, course materials) that you can compile and organize.

- You're creating something simple like a quote collection with photos of your pet.
- You're editing an anthology where others submit content and you arrange it.

If you're smart about the weekend approach, you'd send your compiled manuscript to a professional editor afterward and pay $2,000 to $6,000 to fix the spelling, punctuation, grammar, and redundancies before you publish.

The answer is hell no if:

- You're starting from scratch with original content.
- You want to write anything requiring narrative craft (memoir, novel).
- You expect the result to be anything more than a rough first draft.
- You're naive enough to think quality writing happens in 48 hours.

The weekend warriors who succeed aren't actually writing books in a weekend—they're organizing existing content or creating simple compilations. There's nothing wrong with that approach, but let's call it what it is.

4. What's Your Content Readiness Level?

- **Lots of existing material (blog posts, presentations, courses)**
  If this describes your situation, then go ahead and compile and organize these bits into how-to guides, business books, or inspirational collections.

- **Some existing material but needs development**
  You may have enough to get going on a business book, expert positioning book, or even a memoir.
- **Starting from scratch with expertise**
  Sounds like the makings of a how-to guide, business books, or interview-based book.
- **Starting from scratch without deep expertise**
  You might want to consider an anthology, quote collection, or collaborative project.

If there's one message I'd like you to take away it's this: Stop ignoring content you've already created as if it's worthless because it doesn't have a fancy book cover yet. If you've been blogging, speaking, or teaching in your field, you likely have enough material for a book right now. You're just not seeing it because you're probably busy fantasizing about starting from scratch like some literary pioneer. (Chapter 5, my friend, is just for you.)

Your definition of success should drive your genre choice, not the other way around.

The Most Strategic Genres for Today's Writers

Need some more ideas, or another way of analyzing your choices? Based on my experience with hundreds of clients, here are the genres that consistently deliver results for different goals:

For Expert Positioners and Practical Professionals:

Business Books: Establish authority, attract better clients, generate speaking opportunities

Examples: *Good to Great* by Jim Collins; *Blue Ocean Strategy* by W. Chan Kim and Renée Mauborgne

How-To Guides: Solve specific problems your audience faces repeatedly

Examples: *The Secrets of Skinny Chicks* by Karen Bridson; *Design Your Self* by Karim Rashid

Expert Positioning Books: Share your methodology and unique approach

Examples: *No Child Left Inside* by Bryn Lottig; *Own Your Niche* by Stephanie Chandler

Workbooks: Interactive guides that walk readers through your process

Examples: *Boundaries Workbook* by Henry Cloud; *The Self-Esteem Workbook* by Glenn Shiraldi

For Influential Storytellers:

Inspirational Books: Combine personal experience with actionable advice

Examples: *The War of Art* by Steven Pressfield; *Simple Grace* by Beth Jannery

Memoirs: Focus on specific transformational periods that offer universal lessons

Examples: *Eat, Pray, Love* by Elizabeth Gilbert; *Traveling Mercies* by Anne Lamott

For Beautiful Writers:

Literary Memoir: More commercial potential than fiction, but requires strong craft skills
Examples: *Educated* by Tara Westover; *Kitchen Confidential* by Anthony Bourdain
Literary Fiction: Artistic recognition but longer timelines and uncertain commercial prospects
Examples: *Little Bee* by Chris Cleave; *Never Let Me Go* by Kazuo Ishiguro

For Any Type of Writer Interested in Quick Market Testing:

Quote Collections: Simple to compile, easy to test
Examples: *Life: Selected Quotes* by Paulo Coelho; *The Little Book of Romanian Wisdom* by Diana Doroftei
Anthologies: Collections of essays or stories by others
Examples: *The Right Words at the Right Time* by Marlo Thomas; *A Blessing in Disguise* by Andrea Joy Cohen

Test Before You Invest

Speaking of testing, here's something that's completely changed the game, yet most writers ignore it as if they're allergic to efficiency: you can validate your book concept (and therefore the genre) before writing it. How about that for making the decision process even easier?!

That LinkedIn post that got thousands of likes? Perfect foundation for a business book. Those how-to videos that generated hundreds of comments asking for more? You've got a proven how-to guide waiting to be written. The personal story you shared that prompted dozens of private messages saying, "How did you know exactly what I needed to hear?" That's potential memoir gold right there.

Testing your content isn't cheating. It's called being smart. And here's the rough dance steps for doing it...

Strategic Testing Approach:

1. Share your core concepts on social media
2. Present your framework at industry events
3. Create a newsletter series around your main ideas
4. Offer a mini-course or workshop on your topic

The content that generates the strongest response tells you exactly what your audience wants from your book.

Skip the Romantic Nonsense

Let me address some common genre misconceptions I hear that waste people's time and keep them stuck in perpetual planning mode:

> *I want to write a novel because it sounds more prestigious than a business book.*

Listen, if your goal is professional credibility, a novel won't serve you unless you're Stephen King. And last I checked;

Stephen King didn't become successful by writing business books first.

> *I should write a comprehensive big idea book because that's what thought leaders do.*

Most people don't have enough original research or insights for a 300-page big idea book. You know what serves readers better and establishes expertise faster? A focused how-to guide that solves an actual problem they're facing right now.

> *Memoir sounds easier than fiction because it's just my life.*

Oh, honey. Memoir requires the same narrative craft skills as fiction, plus the additional challenge of working within the constraints of truth and not pissing off your entire family.

> *I'll write something literary to prove I'm a real writer.*

Real writers serve their readers and achieve their goals. Genre snobbery helps no one, and it definitely doesn't pay your mortgage.

Find Your North Star Book

Ready to take your first leap? Once you've answered the strategic questions and chosen your genre, find one book that represents exactly what you want to create. This becomes your model—not something to copy, but something to reverse-engineer.

Study how the author structured their content, what tone they used, how they engaged their target audience, and what made readers respond. This becomes your roadmap. (I'll be diving deep into book-model analysis in Step Three; don't you worry.)

For business professionals, find a book that establishes someone as an authority in your field. For storytellers, find a memoir whose approach resonates with your vision. This isn't about plagiarism; it's about understanding what works.

Stop Making This Complicated

Here's what I see too often, and it makes me want to stage an intervention: writers spending months researching genres, reading dozens of books in different categories, attending conferences about genre selection, joining Facebook groups to debate the merits of various approaches, and basically doing everything except making a damn decision and writing something.

Stop!

Pick your genre based on your goals, skills, and timeline. There are no mistakes here—only learning experiences and, occasionally, pivot opportunities. The worst thing you can do is never start because you're hobbled by choice and convinced there's some perfect genre waiting to be discovered if you just research long enough.

If you're still straddling the genre fence after reading this chapter, here's my prescription: default to prescriptive nonfiction. How-to guides, business books, and expert positioning books serve clear audiences, have proven structures, and offer the best return on investment for most authors' goals. Plus, they don't require you to channel your inner Hemingway or bare your soul to strangers.

Your book should serve your broader professional goals, not just satisfy your desire to be published. Pick the genre that gets you where you want to go, then get started.

DO THIS

1. Answer the four strategic questions above and let them guide your decision.
2. Choose one genre based on your writer type and goals—no hedging or "maybe both."
3. Find and buy your North Star book within one week of making your genre decision.
4. Test your core concept with your existing audience before committing to the full manuscript.
5. Remove one time sink from your weekly schedule to create your writing block.
6. Stop researching genres and start writing in your chosen one.

4

THE WRITING PROCESS, FOR REALZ

What Really Happens When You Sit Down to Write

Before we set to work creating and gathering content, I'd like to pause, take a deep breath, and talk about the writing process. Believe me, you'll want to know what to expect so you can recognize the obstacles for what they are: inevitable pains in the ass. You'll want to know that what you're experiencing is normal, not some sign that you're doing something horribly wrong.

Most aspiring writers have pretty glamorized notions about how this whole thing works. They think they'll sit down, channel their inner literary genius, and spin pure gold on the first try. Then, they wonder why they feel like horrible failures when reality hits.

The biggest idealized notion? That you can write a perfect book in one try. Well, let me take a hatchet to that fantasy right here and now.

The One Draft Mentality

Beware the One Draft Mentality: That crazy notion that allows one to believe that a story can be captured on paper in one fell swoop. This perfectionistic, crippling mindset will prevent nice people like you from moving on to paragraph two before the next millennium.

Simply put, in order to write a book, you'll need to write several drafts, not just one, so do yourself a favor and get over it.

But here's the good news: your only job at this point is to write the first draft, the first shitty draft. This is the big hurdle. The rest, relatively speaking, is cake. While you work on your shitty first draft, do not play with your wording, polish your verbs, or restructure your sentences. Do not edit in the field, as landscape photographers say. Write. Just write. Get the stuff down as fast as it'll come. Because chances are really good that you're going to chop your first four chapters or the first four pages of each chapter before you're done. Don't waste time on things that will likely go bye-bye.

To anchor my point, I want to tell you a little story about my daughter, Iman, and her One Draft Mentality. I'm going to paint a scene because, as we'll discuss, scenes are what readers remember.

Once upon a time, Iman came home for semester break with a 25-page paper due the day she was to return to class. True to her nature, Iman left her project until the very last minute.

Stressed, she sat at the kitchen counter facing a blank piece of paper. She'd write one sentence, then think for ten minutes. She'd get up and pace, then sit back down to cry. Wiping her nose, she'd write the next belabored sentence before beginning the cycle again. This went on for hours. Bent over, her long, curly hair wet with tears, her tiny face pressed into hands no bigger than a baby's, she said, in response to my incredulous expression, "Mom, you don't understand. I don't have time to get this wrong."

See, Iman believed that writing multiple drafts of a paper was a waste of time, inefficient. She believed that one should be able to get the job done perfectly in just one go. And to be fair, after fourteen hours of stress, after buckets of tears, she finished her paper, handed it in, and received a decent grade.

Like Iman, you might get away with the One Draft Mentality when writing a 25-page academic paper. Adopt that mindset when writing an entire book, however, and you'll end up in the psychiatric ward of your local hospital.

This is why I'm not only giving you permission to write a shitty first draft; I'm insisting that you do so. Now, when I say "shitty first draft," I'm talking about writing so bad that you'd die of embarrassment if anyone read it, even the dog. Complete this draft first; then, and only then, go back and clean it up.

Listen, if you want to be really good at something, you must be willing to be bad in the beginning. That's how this thing called *process* works.

And while I'm doling out permission—permission designed to free you up, to allow your creativity to flow without that vicious self-judgment getting in the way—I'd like to offer you more:

I Hereby Give You Permission to Do the Following

- You get to change your mind (after you write your shitty first draft).
- You get to make mistakes.
- You get to vacillate.
- You get to take your own sweet time.
- You get to speak your mind.
- You get to be direct and honest.
- You get to fail.
- You get to be wrong.
- You get to be "unreasonable."
- You get to shine.
- You get to disengage yourself from problems you cannot immediately solve.
- You get to play big.
- You get to ask for help.
- You get to be imperfect.
- You get to be free.
- You get to love yourself.
- You get to leave things alone.
- You get to experiment.
- You get to question the *status quo.*
- You get to have things the way you want them.
- You get to rock the boat.
- You get to be the wonderful, quirky you.

Now that I've given you permission to be human, let me share some reality about what becoming a skilled writer actually requires. Because while I want you to embrace imperfection, I also want you to understand what you're signing up for.

The Cold Hard Truth

For some strange reason, whenever I conducted a beginners' writing workshop back in the day, one of my students invariably raised her hand and gushed on about her desire to write novels just like Jane Austen's. Jane Austen, I insisted on mentioning, did not roll out of bed one morning at the tender age of twenty-five and write *Pride and Prejudice* in one go.

Prodigy or not, here are a few things you, too, should probably know about Jane Austen and what she did to produce some decent books:

- She wrote stories from the time she was a young child.
- She lived in her parents' home until she died at forty-one, never having married.
- Her family had money, so Jane could spend her days writing in her bedroom, not darning socks.
- She wrote multiple drafts of her novels and discarded hundreds, if not thousands, of pages before she produced her masterpieces.
- Her masterpieces weren't considered masterpieces until long after her death.
- Jane Austen put in over 10,000 hours at her desk to become a master.

(For those of you who do not want to put in 10,000 hours to create a decent book, we'll be talking about editing services later.)

Note: In his book *Outliers*, Malcolm Gladwell theorizes that true mastery—mastery of any skill—requires 10,000 hours of practice. In other words, no one comes out of the box writing like John Updike. Now, I'm not convinced that 10,000 hours is a prerequisite for a great book, but I do know that you need to give yourself permission to wrestle with this thing.

Stay with me while I expand on this topic.

Have you ever watched a professional runner run? Looks so easy, doesn't it? They've all got that half-smile playing across their faces, that healthy sheen, those long, fluid strides that make the act seem so fun. You can practically feel the endorphins pumping through your body from the couch.

Inspired, you go out for a jog and discover that, instead of gliding like Flo Jo across the savannah, with the wind whipping through your hair, you're ready to throw up by the end of the block. You shake your head, confused, because you know nothing about the inglorious stages a runner must go through along the way. You figure if something so simple feels so hard, there must be something wrong with you. Clearly, you've inherited your mother's delicate genes, not to mention her chunky thighs, so you might as well stagger back home and take up bridge.

No surprises here; good writing is a lot like good running. There's a lot more to the sport than meets the eye.

Just for a moment, I'd like to lift the skirts on writing and describe, in great detail, the "normal" process—the process that your favorite writers make look so deceptively easy. It's important to know what's really under there so you'll know what to expect. For fun, I'm going to break the process down into thirteen predictable stages or steps.

The 13 Stages of Writing (Yes, It's Always This Messy)

1. You start with a brilliant idea for an essay or a chapter, and you can hardly wait to get going because you're really excited. You know precisely what you want to say. You can envision the perfect words pouring onto the paper while you sit back with your arms folded and witness the magic.

2. Grinning, you sketch out the story of a man you met who changed your life. Maybe you don't know exactly how he changed your life, but you recall all the memorable details: how you met, what he looked like, what he said, what you said, even the kind of cologne he wore. Lots and lots of great details.

3. You write page after page until you reach the end and are ready to draw a conclusion. This man changed my life because...because...

4. You think back, and you're suddenly not sure how he changed your life, that he even did, why you chose to write about him in the first place, or what anything you wrote about means when push comes to shove. A trickle of sweat slides down your neck.

5. After you get your third glass of water, or eat the contents of your refrigerator, you sit back down and think

some more. What was the point? Because there is a God in heaven and (s)he is merciful, you suddenly realize the story is about something else entirely, something crucial. You just need to change a few things now and get rid of some stuff supporting the original aborted idea. You had no idea you were such a genius!

6. You flesh out your new point. It's really good.

7. Then you go back to the beginning of the piece, and you realize that the story *really* starts on page four, which means you've got to cut those first four pages off—the ones, let's be honest, that took so damn much effort and time to write. Because you don't waste, and we'll talk more about this later, you stick those extraneous pages in the scrap heap, a separate file in your computer labeled as such, and continue on your way.

8. When you've got your story down and feel satisfied, you stick the draft in the bottom drawer. Even though you've been told not to edit in the field—not to go back and incessantly toy with your wording before your shitty first draft is done—you're going to ignore my instructions and go back in to reevaluate instead of pushing forward on your next story.

9. At first glance, you think that what you've got in hand looks pretty damn good. You're a natural. A genius. Oh, how you snort.

10. The next day, however, because you *really* can't follow instructions, you look at it again. You can't believe what's happened! Seemingly overnight, some cruel six-year-old got into your document and turned your

brilliance into complete and utter shit. You weep. Profusely. And threaten to quit.

11. On Wednesday—always on Wednesday—you fix a few things because you just can't move on. Just because you have nothing better to do, now that you're a total, irredeemable failure, you slip in that random idea that popped into your head when you were picking up the dry cleaning, the one you should have written down in your story notebook instead. And suddenly, the project, once again, kicks to life.

12. Finally, on Thursday, you figure your piece is good enough, once again, to move on to the next section. You keep your head down, and you claim, should anybody ask, that you'd never edit in the field because you understand your goal is to push forward so you can complete a shitty first draft full of horrors and mistakes. You bristle at the suggestion you could be so stupid.

13. And to make a long, sad story short, by the time you finish your final draft—that draft you'll mail out for publishing—you will have thrown out half of your chapters or cut out enormous chunks of brilliance from one area and moved them to another. And that book of yours—its structure, message, tone—is nothing like what you envisioned in the beginning. It looks almost nothing like your shitty first draft, that draft you had to write to get to this point.

Here's the good news, the take-home message: You do not have to write a perfect first draft like Iman. You don't even need to write a good one. In fact, consider it your job to write a *Truly Shitty First Draft*. Because you just have to start.

You must start somewhere, or you never get anywhere.

Before You Get Carried Away

I want to remind you of a number of other important concepts. As your writing advisor, I see it as my job to give you an occasional tap on the nose to ensure you've got (and keep) your head in the game.

Ready?

- **You're a writer. That means you need to read other writers.** Turn off the TV and read!
- **The only way to begin is simply to begin.** I wish it were more complicated.
- **Tell the story in the first format that occurs to you.** If, after you've finished your first draft, it seems wrong to have told your life story in the how-to form, then turn it into something else. But only after you've finished. Trust me on this one: nothing is a waste.
- **Writing is a pleasure.** A little luxury. Like eating an ice cream sundae without the calories. You can buy into the "it's-so-damn-hard" mindset, but you're only wasting precious energy and time. Coal mining is hard; writing, not so much. Let's keep this in perspective.
- **You get to do this. Look around.** Nobody is holding a gun to your head. I hope.
- **Trust in the process.** And we're going to talk a lot more about the process. Every first draft, no matter

who creates it, looks like garbage. It will get better. This is the starting point. Your book will change over time.

About That Motivation Thing

This is going to come up. I just know it will....

Do you need to be motivated to take action? Hell no. In fact, there are lots of times you'll absolutely not feel like taking action when you promised yourself you would sit down and write. I'm here to tell you these very moments are the moments you'll need to take action anyway. Otherwise, you'll stand around filing your nails while the world passes you by.

I love writing; I really do, but I'd rather clean toilets than sit down to face a blank page. Actually, I'd rather trot down to the kitchen and eat the pan of raw vegan brownies my client just FedExed over. And I'd rather dig into season two of *Succession* on Netflix, which I've just discovered, and forget about the fact that I don't have a clue what I'm going to say next, preferably with the aforementioned brownies. But I digress.

Motivation, i.e., good feelings, is not required to take action. You act anyway, regardless of how uninspired you feel. Think of motivation as a perk, sort of like popcorn at the movies. It's nice to have, particularly with a crapload of salt and butter, but not necessary to enjoy the show.

More often than not, motivation arises after you start, after you get going. After you start to write and get in the flow. And suddenly, you don't know why you didn't want to start earlier. You feel good; you're motivated; you're on fire. The motivation and the good feelings follow the action.

Here's the funny thing: motivation and action are co-arising phenomena. One doesn't necessarily precede the other. Sometimes, like when you've got lots of time and space, you can hardly wait to get going. Sometimes, you can write for an hour, and it feels like a day. That happens. It will happen.

When Motivation Fails You

So, how do you take action during block time when you don't really feel like it or if the motivation hasn't come somewhere during the process?

- **Remember your why:** Why you're working on this book in the first place. Dial back into the goal, the vision, the destination. The very reason you decided action was required in the first place. Connect regularly with your why.

- **Decide you're going to do something once**—like write for two hours three times a week. Don't revisit your decision to act; don't complain; don't rethink; don't reevaluate. Just do it.

- **Make it a habit; make it routine.** Write from 9 p.m. to 11 p.m. on Thursday and Saturday nights. Be predictable. And boring. It's good for you.

- **Stop waiting around for the perfect moment, when you feel like it.** For all of the planets to align and the angels to show up singing a show tune. The people who are getting the results you want? Who are doing the things you wish you could be doing? They're not riding the motivation pony, man. They're following a routine and doing the things they don't feel like doing. That's just how it works.

Now, all of this—the messy process, the multiple drafts, the need for discipline—that's the same whether you're writing in 1925 or 2025. The fundamentals of good writing haven't changed. But here's what's different now, and why it actually makes the process more manageable for strategic writers...

The New Rules

Returning to the point I've already made and will probably make 457 times more: the publishing landscape has completely transformed, and that's actually good news for writers like you. You have more options than ever before, but you also have more competition for readers' attention.

The writers who succeed in today's market understand that the writing process—this messy, sometimes frustrating process—is just the beginning. You'll also need to think about building an audience, creating a platform, and connecting with readers. But here's the thing: all of that starts with having something worth reading.

That's why the process matters more than ever. Readers have endless choices now. They can find books on any topic, in any genre, at any price point. What makes them choose your book over the thousands of others published daily? Quality. Authenticity. A voice that speaks directly to them.

You develop that voice by going through this process—by writing that shitty first draft and then making it better.

Now, this doesn't mean you share your raw first draft with the world. There's a difference between your private shitty first draft and the content you test publicly. Your first draft is for your eyes only; it's where you get the ideas out of your head and onto the page without judgment. But once you've written that terrible first version, you can pull out the good ideas, clean them up just enough to be coherent, and test those concepts with your audience.

Think of it this way: your shitty first draft is like cooking in your kitchen with the door closed. You're going to make a mess, burn some things, and probably create a few disasters. But when you invite people over to taste-test, you've at least made sure the food is edible and presented on clean plates. You're not serving them your kitchen disasters, but you're also not waiting until you're a Michelin-starred chef.

The content you share publicly should be clear enough to communicate your ideas but rough enough that you can still refine it based on feedback. A LinkedIn post about a concept from Chapter 4 doesn't need to be perfect prose; it needs to be clear, valuable, and engaging enough to generate meaningful responses.

The Method Behind the Madness

Heed my words: the book you set out to write this first go-round will not be the same book you end up with when you're done. You are, therefore, wasting your precious time fiddling with things as you move along. Get the ideas down, as rough as they are, and push forward. Don't edit in the field.

Remember, nothing is a waste—time, effort, those beautiful words you struggled to come up with or received as a gift from the Universe. It's all part of the process.

You don't get to skip to the front of the line. You don't get to run like Flo Jo before placing 155th in your town's annual 5K. You don't get to write *Pride and Prejudice* without creating, first, an awful lot of crap. Everyone goes through this sequence, this process, including Jane Austen.

And here's something else: in today's publishing world, going through this process properly gives you a competitive advantage. While other people rush to publish their first drafts, you'll be putting out work that's been through the refining fire. That matters to readers, and it matters to your long-term success as an author. To success!

DO THIS

1. Copy these words in black magic marker—the bigger, the better: My J-O-B is to write a shitty first draft. Now hang them on the wall next to your computer.

2. Create a Scrap Heap folder on your computer. This is where the stuff you chop will end up. There will be excess, guaranteed.

3. Make a mistake this week. Tell people about it. Notice how you feel. Have a good laugh. Think about how you might do it differently next time.

4. Give yourself permission to be imperfect during this process. That's not giving up; that's being strategic.

5. Remember that every successful author you admire went through this exact same process. They just don't talk about it much because it's not very glamorous.

5

THE SCAVENGER HUNT

Mine Your Existing Content Before Creating New Material

Enough philosophy; let's get to work. Ready to start generating content for your book? Yah? Well, hold on for a sec. Before we create brand new material, seemingly out of thin air, we're going to identify some useful tidbits you may already have lying around the house. Look around. What are you ignoring?

Let me show you exactly what I mean by starting with the master class in content repurposing.

Want to see content repurposing done by someone who knows what they're doing? Look at what Tim Ferriss did with *Tools of Titans*. After conducting nearly 200 interviews on *The Tim Ferriss Show*—generally the most popular business podcast on iTunes—Ferriss had thousands of pages of transcripts and hand-scribbled interview notes.

Now, the amateur move would have been to slap those transcripts together, add an introduction and conclusion, and call it a book. What a disorganized, unreadable disaster that would have been. And yet, that's exactly what many podcasters would probably do because they don't understand the difference between content and a book.

Instead, Ferriss did the hard work that separates professionals from wannabes. He sifted through all that material to unearth the gems, then organized it into a 673-page masterpiece that became a bestseller. He divided his content into three main sections: Healthy, Wealthy, and Wise. Each interview subject got a concise bio with compelling visual elements and key quotes. But here's the crucial part—he didn't just dump entire interview transcripts like some doobie bent on getting things done and dusted. He pulled out the questions that elicited the most interesting answers, made them bold subheadings, and then provided distilled responses below.

Ferriss then drew attention to patterns and commonalities—habits, beliefs, and recommendations that successful people shared. The themes that wouldn't have been obvious in individual interviews emerged: delay gratification, get comfortable with the uncomfortable, pursue happiness over financial success.

The result? A book that feels cohesive despite being compiled from hundreds of separate conversations.

That synthesis work separates professional authors from people who think publishing means dumping content into a document and calling it a day.

Now, before you start feeling intimidated by the Ferriss example, let me bring this down to earth for you. You might not have 200 podcast interviews sitting around, but I can all but guarantee you're sitting on your own treasure trove and don't even know it. You've been creating material for years—blog posts, presentations, social media snippets, client communications, training materials... The question isn't whether you have content; it's whether you're smart enough to recognize it and professional enough to synthesize it properly.

Not sure what I mean? Let me give you some examples that'll either inspire you or make you want to kick yourself for missing obvious opportunities.

The content landscape has exploded into a feeding frenzy beyond anything we could have imagined back in the day. Today's successful authors are mining material from everywhere—TikTok videos, LinkedIn articles, podcast transcripts, YouTube channels, online course materials, and even Instagram stories. Meanwhile, far less savvy writers are still staring at blank pages like deer in...no, I refuse to use yet another cliché.

The point is this: while you've been dismissing your existing content as "not good enough" for a book, successful authors have been systematically mining their archives and turning everyday material into bestsellers. You can too.

A Potential Treasure Trove

Let's start with the most obvious place you're probably overlooking:

Your Digital Footprint

If you've been in business for over five minutes, you've created content. Stop acting like you haven't. That presentation you gave at the industry conference? That's material. The training materials you developed for your team? That's content. The detailed responses you've written to client questions? That's pure book material moldering in your email archives.

Here's what drives me crazy about most professionals: you've been road-testing your ideas in real time and don't even realize it. Every presentation that received great audience engagement, every training module that clicked with participants, every client conversation that led to a breakthrough—that's market-tested material just waiting to be turned into book content.

Social Media Riches

LinkedIn has become the new blogging platform for professionals, which is why you're hearing me drone on about it. If you've been active there, you're sitting on a content mother lode. Those thought leadership posts that garnered hundreds of comments? The industry insights that sparked heated debates? The case studies you shared? All perfect jumping-off points for book chapters. I've seen authors turn viral LinkedIn posts into entire book chapters because the engagement showed them exactly what resonated with their audience.

(By the way, Chapter 10 is all about stringing blog posts together into a compelling book. So, wait for it.)

Facebook posts, Twitter threads, and even well-crafted Instagram captions can also spark ideas or provide the seed for larger stories. Stop dismissing this as "just social media."

Did you know that the outrageously popular book *Sh*t My Dad Says* started from a Twitter stream? (Yes, X—formerly Twitter, now the Wild West of social media, though I'll probably keep calling it Twitter because that feels saner.) Moving back to his parents' house after a disastrous relationship, Justin Halpern started tweeting about the ridiculous things his father said, things that would have otherwise driven poor Justin to drink. These tweets quickly drew the attention of a huge fan base, followed shortly by a major publishing house.

Which reminds me...Here's something most authors are clueless about: agents and editors are constantly trolling social media, looking for content that takes off. They're hunting for ideas, voices, and audiences that already exist. You should be doing the same thing—scanning for great book ideas. This is especially helpful if that content drawing massive attention happens to be yours.

Podcasts

Remember the Ferriss model from our opening example? He transcribed every conversation and systematically mined those transcripts for insights. You can do the same thing, even if you've never been on a podcast—record yourself answering the questions you get asked most often, transcribe it, and mine it for the good stuff. Set up your phone, hit record, and pretend you're being interviewed. You'll generate hours of usable material in an afternoon.

Video Content

YouTube videos, training recordings, webinar presentations, and even those Zoom calls where you shared your screen and explained your methodology—all of this can be repurposed. The spoken word might need heavy editing to work on the page, but the ideas, examples, and frameworks are already there.

I know a pair of consultants who turned their signature webinar series—one they ran for their membership program—into a bestselling business book. (Hi, Kelly Higdon and Miranda Palmer, hiiiiiii.) They had the presentations transcribed, pulled out the key points and case studies, and used them as the foundation for their chapters. The book took off because they'd already proven the content worked with live audiences. Meanwhile, other consultants are starting from scratch because they're stone-cold oblivious to what's right in front of them.

Course and Training Materials

If you've created any educational content—online courses, workshop materials, training guides, certification programs—you're sitting on a book bonanza. These materials already have structure, learning objectives, and real-world applications. You've done the heavy lifting of organizing information in a logical sequence.

The beauty of course materials is that they're designed to teach, which means they already have the story-plus-lesson structure that makes for compelling nonfiction books.

But most people act like this content doesn't exist—la-ti-da-di-da—when it comes time to write a book.

Email Marketing Archives

If you've been sending newsletters, email sequences, or regular updates to your list, you've got content assets gathering digital dust while you whine about having nothing to write about. Those emails that generated lots of replies? The ones that prompted people to forward them to colleagues? That's your audience telling you what resonates.

I've seen authors turn their most popular email newsletters into book chapters. The advantage is that you already know which topics generate engagement and which fall flat. Why guess when you have data staring you in the face?

Client Work and Case Studies

This is where it gets really interesting for business professionals and where most people screw up royally. Every client success story, every problem you've solved, every transformation you've facilitated—these are the stories that will make your book compelling instead of theoretical nonsense.

Obviously, you need to be careful about confidentiality and get permission where appropriate. However, with proper disguising and client consent, these real-world examples become the proof points that turn theoretical advice into credible guidance. Yet most professionals act like their client work is off-limits for their book. Ridiculous.

Alright, enough examples of what other people are doing. Time to get systematic about your own content archaeology.

The Digital Scavenger Hunt Process

Here's how to systematically mine your existing content without losing your beans:

1. **Start with your most popular pieces.**
    Which LinkedIn posts received the most engagement? Which presentations garnered the best feedback? Which training modules generated the most questions? Popularity is often a reliable indicator of book-worthy content, but most people ignore this obvious signal.

2. **Look for themes and patterns.**
    If you keep returning to the same concepts in different formats, that's your brain telling you these ideas matter. Those recurring themes often become your book's main chapters. However, you have to pay attention instead of treating each piece of content as if it were an isolated event.

3. **Search your email for the questions you are asked repeatedly.**
    If clients and colleagues keep inquiring about the same issues, your book should definitely address them. This is market research handed to you on a silver platter.

4. **Review your speaking topics.**
    What do event organizers ask you to present on? What topics do audiences respond to most enthusiastically?

Your speaking experience is market research for your book, but most people treat it like entertainment.

Don't Just Copy and Paste

Here's what you need to get through that beautiful skull: repurposing doesn't mean copying and pasting like some lazy content farmer. A LinkedIn post might spark a chapter idea, but it won't become a chapter without significant development. A presentation might provide the framework, but you'll need to add stories, examples, and deeper insights.

Think of your existing content as clay, not a finished sculpture. It's the raw material you'll shape into something new and valuable. Remember Tim Ferriss—he didn't just publish transcripts. He mined, distilled, synthesized, and reorganized until he had something cohesive and useful.

Most people skip this crucial step because it requires actual work. I know! I hate work, too!

Speaking of work, here's your comprehensive checklist so you don't miss anything obvious while you're digging around.

Stop-Making-Excuses-and-Start-Looking Checklist

Professional Materials:

1. Presentation slides and speaker notes
2. Training manuals and workshop materials
3. Client onboarding documents

4. Standard operating procedures
5. Industry white papers you've written
6. Conference presentations and handouts

Digital Content:

1. Blog posts and articles
2. LinkedIn articles and posts
3. Podcast appearances (get transcripts)
4. Video content and webinars
5. Online course materials
6. Email newsletters and sequences

Communication Archives:

1. Frequently asked client questions
2. Detailed email responses to common problems
3. Social media posts that generated engagement
4. Interview responses (written or transcribed)
5. Speaking bureau biography and topic descriptions

Turn Your Mess into Something Useful

Once you've gathered your content, you'll need to transform it from its original format into book material. A tweet might become a chapter opening, a case study might become the backbone of an entire section, and a presentation might provide the structure for multiple chapters.

The key is recognizing that you're not starting from scratch like some poor innocent with no experience. You're building on a foundation of proven ideas and tested content. But, again, remember the Ferriss lesson: the magic happens in the synthesis. Heed my warning: don't just compile—distill, organize, and find the patterns that create a cohesive message.

Also...Don't try to use everything you find just because you found it. Be selective and ruthless. Choose the content that best serves your book's purpose and your readers' needs. Some of your material will be outdated, some off-topic, and some won't be strong enough for book inclusion.

That's fine. Better to have too much good material than too little. You can always save the extras for your next book or use them for promotional content.

How Long This Actually Takes

This scavenger hunt process, by the way, might take several focused sessions, but it's time well spent compared to staring at blank pages for months. You're essentially doing market research on yourself, identifying what works and what doesn't, what resonates and what falls flat.

Most authors who skip this step end up staring at blank pages longer than necessary, wondering why writing feels impossible. You'll be starting with a pile of tested material and proven ideas—a massive advantage that most writers would kill for.

In other words: Stop making this harder than it needs to be.

DO THIS

1. Set aside a whole day to conduct your content scavenger hunt—don't half-ass this.
2. Create folders for different types of content: presentations, social media, client materials, etc.
3. Look for patterns and themes across different content types—this is where the real value lies, not in individual pieces.
4. Identify your most popular and engaging pieces—these often translate well to book content.
5. Remember: you're looking for raw material to synthesize, not finished chapters to copy and paste.

STEP 2

CREATING
A SHITTY FIRST DRAFT

6

ONE BRICK AT A TIME

Turn Your Raw Material into Compelling Stories

Now that you've identified your content treasure trove, it's time to transform it into the kind of material that actually sticks in readers' minds. Here's what I suspect—in fact, I'd bet dollars to donuts on this—most of your existing content is missing the one element that makes ideas memorable: compelling stories with faces readers can connect to.

But first, let me explain exactly what we're building here.

Think of your book as a brick house. You can't build a brick house without a generous supply of bricks, no matter how gifted you are with a buttering trowel. The same goes for your book—you need individual pieces of solid content before you can worry about how they all fit together.

I call these individual pieces "bricks" because they're the sturdy building blocks that support your entire book. Each brick is a self-contained piece of content that serves a specific purpose. Some bricks teach a concept through frameworks or systems. Others provide proof through case studies or data. But the most important bricks—and the ones we're focusing on first—are story bricks.

Why Story Bricks Come First

Whether you're writing a business book, memoir, or how-to guide, readers get lost without supporting stories. If you make an important point, you've got to support it with a story, or you'll lose your reader. They'll wander off to check Instagram or order a matcha latte and never come back.

Think about it. Have you ever picked up a business book and found yourself bored to tears within five minutes? The author may have made excellent points, but the whole thing read like a dry textbook. Tell me you didn't throw that book down. Want to know the fatal flaw? Yup! It lacked stories.

Here's the thing: readers crave stories with faces they can attach to and sensory details. According to neuroscience research, our brains light up when we read about smells, sounds, tastes, touch, and sights. It's what our minds want. Those details keep us grounded and turning pages.

The Building Blocks You'll Create

The next step you'll need to take—ignoring all the rest that lie ahead—is to form a single, tiny brick of material. What do I mean by "brick"? Depending on the genre you've chosen, I'm talking about one of the following:

- One blog post (enhanced with story elements)
- One scene (for memoir or fiction)
- One case study (told as a narrative)
- One expanded, supported idea (with supporting stories)
- One client transformation (told with characters and plot)
- One lesson learned the hard way (dramatized as a scene)
- One "aha" moment that changed everything (shown, not just told)
- One clear teaching point (illustrated through human examples)

Notice how each of these needs story elements to work? Even a business case study needs characters (the client), setting (their situation), plot (the problem and solution), and ideally some dialogue and sensory details to make it memorable.

We're focusing on stories because they're the hardest part to write and the most essential element across all genres.

How to Write a Simple Story

I'm going to walk you through my story-writing process using an example from my memoir. But follow along even if you're writing a case study for a business book—the same storytelling principles apply across all genres.

Before we dive in, let me clarify: when I say "story," I'm using it as an umbrella term covering both full stories and anecdotes. A story typically has a complete narrative arc with a beginning, middle, and end. An anecdote is shorter and more focused, usually capturing a single moment that illustrates a point. Both serve the same purpose in your book: they make abstract concepts concrete and give readers faces to connect with.

Finding Your Story Seed

It's Tuesday morning, my scheduled writing block time, and I'm staring at a blank page. I browse through my story notebook looking for an idea that's been swirling around in my head. Here are a few notes I jotted down:

1. I heard that song in a restaurant: "I'll Take You Home Again, Kathleen." It made me want to run away. It was the song Dad loved to play on his violin.

2. I had a conversation with a friend about feeling like I was being held hostage when my husband took too long to answer questions. My friend asked, "Did anybody else ever make you feel you were being held hostage?" And I remembered my dad—how he would wake me up in the middle of the night to wash dishes while he ranted about his miserable life.

There it is—that "hostage" feeling I've been mulling over. This reminds me of a specific story: my dad dragging me into the kitchen in the middle of the night. I'm going to dramatize this moment to explore the idea of being held hostage.

Here's my broad statement: Sometimes, for no apparent reason, I feel trapped. Like I'm being held hostage. I'm going to type this at the top of my page as a writing prompt.

Building the Story Structure

Here's the path I'll follow:

I'm going to place my ten-year-old self in the kitchen with my father.

I could bring my mother and brother into the story, but I don't want to complicate things. I'm going to leave them sleeping in their beds.

I'm going to set our story in the kitchen. Dad will have already pulled me out of bed. I want my readers to be in that kitchen with me.

I'm going to illustrate everything that I see because my readers want to see what I do. I'm going to describe the stack of dirty dishes on the counter, the open cabinet door above the sink—the one I always bump my head on—the tub of Country Crock margarine with the toast crumbs swirled on the surface by the refrigerator, and the yellow plastic dishpan in the sink. I'm going to give you a glimpse of my pajama sleeve as it soaks up dishwater and my dad's short-sleeved white dress shirt, an intermittent flash in my peripheral vision.

Then, I'm going to mention what I smell because readers want to smell what I do. I'm going to note the whiskey on my father's breath, the smell of three-hour-old spaghetti sauce on the stovetop, the grease from the frying pan, and the sweet stench of the guinea pig cage that's sitting on a stool in the corner.

I'm going to describe what I hear: the ticking of the ceramic clock my mom painted in class, the refrigerator's hum, and the creak of the bedroom door—my brother's—because he wants to keep an ear open in case the evening escalates.

So, here we are—Dad and me—in this kitchen. You, the reader, are in the kitchen, too. You can see, hear, and smell what I do. You can even feel the grease in the lukewarm dish-water where my shaking hands are. You can feel the sharp knife I cut myself on because I don't know it's there at the bottom of the pan.

Now I need to paint what it feels like to be ten, pulled from my bed and ordered to wash dishes while my combative father looks on. What it feels like to be trapped in the kitchen with no easy way out. Because to leave means to bring something really bad—what is it? I'm not sure—down on my head. I need to show you, my reader, what it feels like to be trapped by an angry, frustrated, heartbroken man who needs to get the pain off his chest when he doesn't know who else to talk to. Who chooses a child instead of his wife because she's already shut him out and will only make him feel worse.

How do I do that?

My first draft will be shitty; first drafts always are. This child will be an innocent victim. The father will be a mon-ster. I'm going to be okay with that for now because this story is seen through the eyes of a child who has no fundamental understanding of the world. The piece will soften up during revision. Right now, I want to get the situation down on paper. I want to capture a feeling. I want my readers to understand and feel trapped, too.

What will my father say to get the action rolling? We need dialogue. We need to hear his voice. "Do you think it's fair that I work all goddamned day, then I have to come home and wash the dishes too at 10:30 at night?" Maybe that's not exactly what he said—after all, this is fifty years ago—but that's pretty close. That's how he sounded. That's about the right feel, the right impact.

And this little girl is going to say something to calm him down, to make herself small so he won't take out his rage on her. "I'm sorry. I didn't know there were dishes in the sink."

I'm going to have a dialogue going, but I'm also going to mention the actions and the body language of our two characters. I'm going to show you how my father sat at the edge of a worn-out stool, his glassy and unfocused eyes, the clenched jaw, the way his hands shook, and how he smoothed that patch of salt-and-pepper hair over his bald spot. Dad is going to get up, pace, scoop the guinea pig from its cage, pace some more, and sit back down. I'm going to focus on him primarily because we're seeing this moment through my ten-year-old eyes. We're seeing this through my point of view.

I'm going to build the tension because readers crave tension. I'll show you how Dad jumped up from the stool as if he were ready to collar me by my pajamas and throw me out into the cold; then, just as quickly, how he controlled his inexplicable rage by pacing that unswept floor and by sitting back down and stroking that guinea pig on his lap instead.

I'll let you hear how he changes the subject from the goddamned dishes to his horrible boss at work, who took all the credit for his airplane engine part design. I'll let you hear my interior dialogue, what I'm saying to myself, what I'm thinking.

Can I leave yet? Is he calm enough for me to go back to bed? Or is it too early? Will I bring his fury down on my head?

After two or three pages, I'll have shown you, my reader, what being trapped looks, smells, sounds, and feels like—maybe even tastes like, if I can also capture that sense. Then, I'm going to end my story. I'm going to leave these two people in the kitchen without any resolution because I'm after the feeling—trapped, held hostage—not a clear conclusion.

What Makes a Story Actually Work

The basic elements I used in that story are:

Characters: Two people with physical descriptions that emphasize the emotional dynamic—Dad's white shirt and bald spot, my wet pajamas.

Setting: A messy suburban kitchen with mundane objects and unique details, like the guinea pig cage, that stick in readers' minds.

Plot: Action is happening—girl is dragged from bed, washing dishes, father is ranting and pacing. Characters need to be doing something; they can't be talking heads.

Dialogue: Characters speak to each other and think in sentence form (inner dialogue). Conversations are non-linear, as they are in real life. Dad says, "I can't stand my boss." The girl replies, "Can I go change? My pajamas got wet?"

Body Language: How bodies move reveals emotion and personality. Dad's nervous hair-swiping, shaking fingers, and hunched shoulders tell you everything about his emotional state.

Sensory Details: The brain lights up when we read about smells, sounds, tastes, touch, and sights. These details keep readers grounded and engaged.

Test Before You Fully Develop

How engaged would the reader be? That's the question. In today's world, I might first post a shorter version of that story online. I'd watch the comments, see what questions people ask, and notice which details spark the strongest response. That feedback becomes invaluable data for developing the full piece.

Post a story on LinkedIn and see if it lands. Tell it in a presentation and watch the audience's reaction. Include it in a blog post and check the engagement.

The stories that get the strongest response become the foundation of your book. The ones that fall flat either get reworked or go into your Spare Brick Pile for later.

This feedback loop didn't exist for previous generations of authors. Use it. Your book will be stronger because you'll know which stories connect with readers before you invest months developing them fully.

Analyze Your Raw Material

Now it's time to pull out that material you organized during your scavenger hunt and see what you're actually working with. This content should be composed of images, ideas, words, perhaps paragraphs or entire posts you grabbed from your resources.

Here are the questions I want you to consider while you skim through these bits:

- What do you have that would constitute a setting?
- Are there any major characters emerging?
- Do you have bits of dialogue?
- Body language?
- What are some of the plot points?
- What kind of movement, action, and activities have you described?
- Which of these story elements seem to be the most fleshed out?
- What sentence, broad idea, character, or object inspires you to begin a story?

See how you've got lots of ideas, concepts, and maybe some good insights? And how you're probably missing the story elements that make content stick in readers' minds?

Tut, tut.

Your job is to take these seeds and develop them into full story bricks using the elements we just covered. That LinkedIn insight needs a human face and a specific setting. That client success needs dialogue and sensory details. That lesson learned needs to be dramatized as a scene with characters doing things.

Don't just tell us, "Client X increased revenue by 40% using our process." Show us Client X (give him a name and a face) sitting in his office (describe it), explaining his problem (let us hear his actual words), and walking through the solution step by step (show the process in action).

Your existing material provides the seed—the insight, the outcome, the lesson. Story elements provide the soil that makes those seeds grow into memorable content. Time to play with this stuff.

Build Your First Brick

Write a story. Take one of your ideas from your scavenger hunt folders and sketch out a scene. Use all the story elements we discussed:

- **Setting:** Where and when does this take place?
- **Character:** Who are the people involved?
- **Plot:** What actions are happening?
- **Dialogue:** What do people say to each other?
- **Body language:** How do their bodies reveal emotion?

Add sensory details—at least one of each kind:

- **Sight:** objects, light and dark, colors, physical details
- **Sound:** tone of voice, footsteps, mechanical sounds
- **Smell:** food, perfume, industrial odors
- **Touch:** hot, cold, furry, ridged, wet
- **Taste:** metal, coffee, fear (yes, emotions have tastes)

Let us be there in that space with you or your character. Paint the scene, develop the tension, and give us people we can connect with.

Remember: you're not starting from scratch. You're taking your proven ideas and insights and giving them the story elements that make content memorable and compelling. Every genre benefits from this approach, whether you're writing memoir, business books, or how-to guides.

The Craft Elements That Hold Everything Together

When the time comes—and you don't need to worry about this while you write your stories—you're going to cement your bricks together with mortar. Just so I don't leave you wondering what the hell I'm talking about; this mortar will include one or a combination of the following:

Exposition: This is when you, the narrator, step out of the scene and summarize what has taken place. For instance, in the Old Testament of the Bible, we learn that the Jews wandered in the desert for forty years. These forty years are described in a couple of paragraphs. We do not stay with the Jews, sandy step by sandy step, for four long decades. The summary of these years gets us to the real action, where the important stuff starts to happen.

Think of exposition as your narrative fast-forward button. Use it to skip over boring but necessary information so you can get to the scenes that matter.

Transitions: Certain words or phrases can help carry a thought from one sentence to another, from one idea to another, or from one paragraph to another. You likely used transitional words—because, however, or furthermore—when you created your first story.

These are the small bridges that keep readers from getting lost as you move between ideas. Without them, your writing feels choppy and disjointed.

Transitional Devices: These link sentences and paragraphs together smoothly so there are no nasty jumps between ideas or points in time. Such devices are handy for joining the main storyline to subplots or backstory. They work by looking backward, reaching forward, and repeating words and ideas. Here are some ways to do that:

Sensory Details: Follow a sound, smell, or taste back and forth through time and place. The smell of coffee in your current kitchen takes you back to Sunday mornings at your grandmother's house.

Objects: A red ball in the present moment trails off into a ball bouncing across the playground when the narrator was a child. The object becomes your time machine.

Dialogue: A character is speaking, but we go back in time to what that person used to say or what someone else once said on that topic. The echo of past conversations informs the present moment, and voilà, we're back in 1969.

Appearance or Setting: While looking at a man with a mustache on the beach, your father suddenly appears in your mind. It's the mustache that reminds you of dear old Dad—or maybe it's the beach itself. You're not sure which, but we follow you there.

However (do you like this transition I'm employing?), let's not lose track of the job at hand, people. We want stories, lots and lots of stories. Lots and lots of other bricks. The mortar doesn't need to be mixed until we finish our shitty first draft. I'm only giving you the heads-up so you can see far enough ahead to settle down and focus on what matters most right now: getting your stories on the page.

Don't get paralyzed trying to perfect your transitions while you're still figuring out what you want to say. Write the content first, then worry about connecting it smoothly.

DO THIS

1. Analyze your scavenger hunt material for story elements. What do you have in spades? What is glaringly absent?

2. Identify your brick type based on your genre. Are you building scenes, case studies, expanded ideas, or client transformations?

3. Choose three pieces of existing material that could be developed into story bricks.

4. Pick one and enhance it with the story elements during your next writing block.

5. Test your story content as you create it. Post shorter versions online, include them in presentations, and add them to newsletters.

6. Build your feedback loop; the stronger the response, the more you know you're onto something worth developing fully.

7

SAME STORY, DIFFERENT GENRE

How One Story Works Across Every Format

So you've written your first story brick following the process I walked you through in Chapter 6. Maybe you've even tested it with your audience and gotten some feedback. Good for you—you're already ahead of most aspiring authors who write in a silo and hope for the best.

But now you might be sitting there thinking, *This story feels too personal for my business book,* or *This seems too simple for my memoir,* or *How the hell does this fit into a how-to guide?*

Stop second-guessing yourself. That story you just created? It's way more versatile than you think.

Here's what most writers don't understand: you don't need completely different stories for different projects. That same core experience can be adapted for a memoir, turned into a case study for a business book, shared as a social media post, or developed into a keynote presentation. Smart writers leverage their best material across multiple formats instead of constantly starting from scratch like some content masochist.

The key is understanding how different genres require different treatments of the same material. My story about feeling trapped in that kitchen with my father? That core emotional experience can work whether I'm writing a memoir, a business book about communication, or a self-help guide about boundary setting. The emotional core stays the same—only the focus, length, and lesson change to match the chosen genre and audience.

Genre Requirements: What Changes and What Stays

Before we dive into specific adaptations, I'm going to repeat an important point: different genres have different requirements. A how-to guide can't be clogged by extraneous details. We don't want Scarlett O'Hara at the top of the spiral staircase when we're trying to understand how to hammer in a nail. Forget the character or the setting in a literary story, however, and you've got yourself a bloody mess.

Here's what drives me crazy: writers who try to force memoir-level detail into business books, or who strip all personality from stories because they think "professional" means "boring." Understanding these requirements helps you choose the right level of detail for your audience, not turn your writing into corporate drone-speak.

How about we take the story I created about my dad and me and drop it into different book genres? I'll spell out the specific requirements so you can apply this to your own material without making a hash of it.

Book Genre Adaptations

Memoir

Unlike autobiographers, memoirists focus on a life-changing chapter rather than life-to-death events. When I began my memoir about living in Iran as a young woman, a story from age ten wouldn't fit the timeline. But every good memoir requires backstory to support current action.

How the kitchen story works: I might place this childhood scene around a current scene where I'm locked in a bedroom after a marital fight. The backstory would illuminate why I react so strongly to feeling trapped, making the current scene more powerful and comprehensible.

Adaptation requirements:

- Rich sensory details and full dialogue
- Complete scene development (2-3 pages)
- Heavy focus on emotional experience and character development
- Must serve the larger narrative arc

Self-Help/Business Book

Readers buy these books to solve specific problems. They want instruction, but even the most motivated will stop reading if you fail to support broad statements with stories that dramatize your point.

How the kitchen story works: It becomes a case study supporting the concept that "People usually overreact when they feel trapped, creating unnecessary conflict in their relationships."

Adaptation requirements:

- Brief subject background: "Ann's father was a mechanical engineer who hated his job...."
- Cut most sensory details, keeping only the most powerful ones for impact.
- Focus on dialogue that has punch.
- Scale down to summarized action while maintaining characters, setting, and key moments.
- Provide clear connection to the business lesson.

Inspirational Book

These books help readers dream and examine different viewpoints, calling them to action through universal themes.

How the kitchen story works: Focus on the universal feeling of being trapped in difficult situations, then extract a lesson that emerges from the experience.

Adaptation requirements:

- Dial back sensory details, choosing only the most memorable (guinea pig cage, father's hair-swiping, knife in dishpan).
- Drive to the heart quickly—no place for escape.
- Turn the specific experience into something universal.
- End with a clear lesson or insight readers can apply.

Personal Essay

Personal essays explore experiences without necessarily proving a point, based on feeling, emotion, and personal experience rather than argument.

How the kitchen story works: Entry point for exploring the theme of being trapped. This could be followed by the bedroom incident or other related experiences.

Adaptation requirements:

- Focus on theme development rather than lesson extraction.
- Allow for exploration and discovery.
- Provide more flexibility in structure and conclusion.
- Permit shifts in direction as themes emerge during writing.

Short Story (Fiction)

Fiction allows you to use real experiences as jumping-off points while inventing new elements.

How the kitchen story works: Maybe Grace (not Ann) isn't smart enough to play it safe and ramps up tension by going back to bed too early. Alternatively, switch perspective to tell it from the father's viewpoint. (Boy, wouldn't that be illuminating!)

Adaptation requirements:

- Stand-alone piece with a beginning, middle, and end.
- Can invent new elements and outcomes.
- May include scenes surrounding the core incident.
- Must have a sense of conclusion.
- Character names and details can be changed.

Your Platform Testing Laboratory

Here's where this gets strategically interesting for book writers, and where most people completely miss the ferry boat: while developing these stories for your book, you can test them across different platforms to see what resonates. This isn't just about building an audience—though that happens—it's about ensuring your book stories actually work before you invest months writing them.

Think about it: every story you're contemplating for your book can be tested in shorter formats. The response tells you which stories have the strongest emotional impact, which lessons resonate most, and which details stick in readers' minds. Use this data to make your book stronger, for crying out loud. Treating your book and your platform as if they're in a custody battle makes zero sense.

Social Media Testing Formats

LinkedIn Article (500-800 words): Focus on the business lesson regarding communication patterns and workplace dynamics. Lead with the universal problem, provide a condensed version emphasizing how childhood patterns manifest in professional settings, and conclude with actionable advice that managers can actually use.

Instagram Post (150 words + image): Use the most visual detail with a powerful opening line: "I was ten years old the first time I learned that some conversations are really monologues in disguise." Follow with the guinea pig cage detail and end with a question that gets people commenting.

Newsletter Story (300-400 words): Use a more intimate tone focusing on emotional insight and relationship lessons. Your subscribers want a personal connection and deeper reflection on how family patterns shape adult behavior.

Twitter Thread (8-10 tweets, 280 characters each): Break into compelling hooks that build tension. Start with: "Thread: The night my father taught me that feeling trapped isn't always about locked doors..." Each tweet should advance the story while building to the insight about communication patterns.

TikTok/YouTube Short (60 seconds): Focus on the most dramatic moment—discovering the knife at the bottom of the dishpan, your father's agitated pacing—and the realization that came years later about family communication patterns. Use visual storytelling with a strong emotional hook.

Presentation Applications

The same story can also become a powerful keynote opening for different topics, and here's where you can really see the versatility at work:

Leadership presentations: "How Leaders Can Recognize When They're Holding Their Teams Hostage." You'd focus on the power dynamics, the one-way conversation, and how leaders sometimes dump their frustrations on subordinates who have no escape route.

Communication workshops: "The Difference Between Sharing and Dumping Emotional Labor." Emphasize how my father wasn't really communicating—he was using me as his personal therapy session without regard for my capacity to handle his problems.

Personal development seminars: "Breaking Generational Patterns That Don't Serve Us." Focus on recognizing inherited communication styles and making conscious choices about how we handle our own frustrations.

Business culture training: "Creating Psychological Safety in Workplace Conversations." Show how feeling trapped in conversations creates the exact opposite of psychological safety and kills honest communication.

In presentation format, start with sensory details to draw the audience in, then pivot to the business application. The story becomes a three-to-four-minute emotional hook that gets everyone leaning forward before you deliver your main content.

Podcast Interview Adaptations

When you're interviewed on different shows, this story becomes your signature example, but here's the smart part—you emphasize different aspects depending on the show's focus.

Parenting Podcast: Focus on the impact on the child and healthy communication modeling. Talk about how children absorb family communication patterns and the importance of age-appropriate emotional boundaries.

Business Podcast: Emphasize workplace communication lessons and leadership insights. Discuss how managers sometimes use employees as sounding boards in ways that create the same trapped dynamic, and what effective leadership communication actually looks like.

Mental Health Podcast: Discuss the long-term effects and healing processes. Explore how childhood experiences of feeling emotionally trapped manifest in adult relationships and what recovery work entails.

Leadership Podcast: Frame it around emotional intelligence and team dynamics. Focus on self-awareness, recognizing when you're dumping versus communicating, and creating genuine psychological safety for your team members.

The beauty of this approach is that you're not memorizing different stories for different shows—you're developing depth around one powerful experience that can serve multiple purposes depending on your audience's needs.

Your Strategic Content Approach

Here's what professional authors do that makes me want to stand on my chair and applaud: they develop five to ten core stories and adapt them to every format they use. Same emotional core, different packaging. This isn't lazy; it's called being smart about your time and energy. So smartttt.

The key is understanding your audience and platform requirements, and this part is crucial:

- **LinkedIn** wants professional insights that don't put people to sleep.
- **Instagram** wants visual, emotional moments that stop the scroll.
- **Newsletters** want personal connection that makes people feel less alone.
- **Keynotes** want universal truths that apply to business without being preachy.
- **Podcasts** want authentic, conversational storytelling that doesn't sound rehearsed.

Post the LinkedIn version and analyze performance. Try the Instagram version and observe engagement patterns. Share it in your newsletter and read the replies. The format that garners the strongest response tells you something crucial about both your audience and the power of your story.

Use this data to refine not just the story but your understanding of what your audience actually wants from you—not what you think they want, but what they demonstrate they want through their responses. The stories that consistently perform well across platforms? Those are the ones that should anchor your book chapters.

The Content Multiplication Effect

When you master story adaptation, you solve multiple problems at once, and I love when things work this efficiently:

1. **Book Development:** You're testing your core content before committing to full chapters.
2. **Platform Building:** You're providing valuable content while writing your book.
3. **Audience Research:** You're learning what resonates with your future readers.
4. **Content Efficiency:** You're getting maximum value from your best material.

Most writers treat their book and their platform as separate projects competing for time and attention. Smart writers figure out they're the same project with different expressions. Stop making this harder than it needs to be.

Remember: Every story you test now makes your book stronger later. You're not just building a platform; you're conducting market research for your manuscript.

DO THIS

1. Study your model book from Chapter 3. Analyze the balance of story elements versus information. How much page space do stories occupy? What level of detail does your genre require?

2. Choose one core story from your content folders—preferably one you've already written or outlined.

3. Adapt your story for three different formats:
   - One book genre (memoir vs. business book vs. inspirational).
   - One social media format (LinkedIn, Instagram, or newsletter).
   - One presentation context (keynote opening or podcast example).

   Pay attention to length requirements, audience expectations, detail level needed, and the main point you're making.

4. Test at least one version with your audience through social media, newsletter, or presentation. Track what resonates and what falls flat.

5. Document the results in your story notebook. Which stories have universal appeal? Which generate the strongest responses? These become your book's foundation stories.

6. Think systematically about your content. You're not creating completely different stories—you're taking the same emotional core and presenting it through different lenses for different purposes.

8

BUT I DON'T WANT TO WRITE A STORY ABOUT YOUR DAD

Seeing Story Adaption in Action

Before I got crazy busy as a publisher, ghostwriter, and content developer, I used to run an online program called Build a Book Bootcamp twice a year. Much of this book's original content was born of that six-week program. Even though I'm an amazing writing coach (the best one on the planet, according to my dog, who should know because he used to eavesdrop on all my classes), students invariably had the same question you probably have right now.

You've identified your content through the scavenger hunt, understand story fundamentals, and know how to adapt stories for different formats. But you might still be wondering: how does this actually work in practice? How do you take everything you've learned and apply it to your specific genre and goals?

My students felt exactly the same way. They understood the story about my dad, grasped the important components, and could see all the genre iterations. Still, they weren't quite sure how to apply the information to their projects. They'd completed their content audit and identified some potential story material, but they felt stuck on the next steps.

The best way to show you how all this works in practice is through real examples. Here are two writers with completely different goals and starting points, and how I'd guide each one through applying our system to their specific challenges.

Crystal and Her Spiritual/ Self-Help Book

Crystal came to me with a spiritual/self-help book idea, though she had a hard time articulating what she was after. Her initial explanation was, shall we say, unclear. As she put it: "I want to write this book because I have a lot to say and share. I want to allow my thoughts, ideas, and insights to flow out of me and come into physical expression. I want something tangible. Rather than just having the experience of speaking, channeling, and providing insights, I want to create a result. Something I can touch and feel and say, 'I created that. I birthed that.' I want to co-create something tangible with the Universe, my Guides, Teachers, and Angels using my Divine Gift of Communication and Authentic Self-Expression. This book will be a how-to of sorts, and it will position me as an expert and be used for my teaching and marketing. However, I'm not sure how much story I'll need. Help!"

See what I mean about unclear? That kind of spiritual word salad tells me everything and nothing at the same time. But buried in there, I could see her real goals: establish expertise, create teaching materials, build a business platform. She just needed help translating her abstract concepts into concrete stories readers could connect with.

So here's what I would say to Crystal if we were sitting together right now, sipping one of those charming bubble teas that seem to have become popular while I wasn't looking.

Start with What You Already Have

First, Crystal, let's look at what you discovered during your content scavenger hunt. You've been doing spiritual coaching for five years, so you've got client transformation stories, presentation materials from workshops, and probably dozens of social media posts about spiritual concepts. That's your foundation.

But here's what I suspect happened when you analyzed that material: lots of abstract concepts, not enough specific human examples. Am I right?

The Strategy for Spiritual/Self-Help Content

This is a spiritual/self-help book, which means your readers are looking for transformation they can believe in. The genre is saturated with people promising enlightenment but delivering recycled platitudes. Your readers have been burned by dozens of books promising spiritual awakening but offering nothing concrete.

This means your stories need to be bulletproof. Every client transformation you write about, every authentic moment you share—these become your credibility. You're not just telling people about transformation; you're showing evidence of it.

Readers want faces they can connect with, people who started where they are and ended up where they want to be. They want to see exactly how the transformation happened.

Mining Your Concepts for Stories

I want to take you through my thought process for how I'd approach your project, Crystal, and what kind of stories I'd begin to develop from your existing material.

First, let's be clear about your story sources. You have two main types of stories to work with: your personal experiences with spiritual concepts and your clients' transformation stories. But think broadly about your personal experiences, Crystal—I'm not just talking about your spiritual awakening moments. I mean your experiences as a human being navigating relationships, career challenges, family dynamics, health scares, and financial stress. All of these can become vehicles for spiritual insights when you connect them to the concepts you teach. Your readers need to see that spiritual principles apply to real-world, everyday situations. Both are essential for a credible spiritual/self-help book.

Do you remember how I focused on the word "trapped" when writing my story? How I was curious about where that particular feeling came from? Well, you've got lots of interesting words to explore in your project description, "authentic" being one of them.

These days, "authentic" gets tossed around like a football. But what does it really mean? What "authentic" means to you may not be what "authentic" means to your readers. Why is this word so important in your work?

Here's how I'd help you mine this concept: Think back to a particular moment when you suddenly realized that being inauthentic was costing you big time—a moment when it was far more painful to pretend to be someone you weren't than to reveal the real you. Then ask yourself:

1. Where were you?
2. Who were you with?
3. What were you saying?
4. What objects, smells, and sights stick out in your mind?
5. What were you experiencing in your body?

Now you're going to paint that picture for your readers, letting them into your world so they know what that experience looks and feels like.

There are probably lots of stories that come to mind for "authentic" alone. You're going to develop them all—two pages here, one page there—until you have a collection of authenticity stories. That's what building a strong first draft is about: having more material than necessary so you can choose the best pieces.

One by one, take on those other concepts you work with—Divine Love, light, truth, abundance—and do the same thing. Because this is the language of your audience, they're familiar with these words, but they don't know what they mean to you or your clients. They don't know the stories behind these words. Once they do, they'll not only understand the words differently; they'll understand themselves in a new way.

Your Client Transformation Stories

But here's where your book really comes together, Crystal: the client stories from your scavenger hunt material. These become your case studies.

I want you to focus on your clients' transformation stories, showing the "before" and "after" pictures while demonstrating how you bridged that gap. What did their life look like before they understood their spiritual gifts? What specific pain were they experiencing? Then, what did you do or say to facilitate their discovery process? Finally, what did the transformation look like once they crossed to the other side?

Think in terms of problems and solutions—they had the problem; you provided the solution. This positions you as the expert while giving readers a roadmap they can follow.

Marcus and His Business Parable

Now let me show you how this same story-focused approach works for a completely different genre and audience. Marcus came to me with business consulting expertise but faced the opposite challenge from Crystal—he was crystal clear about his message but wasn't sure how to make complex business concepts engaging.

Marcus had fifteen years of consulting experience helping companies build sustainable growth strategies. During his
content scavenger hunt, he found presentation after presentation about the same patterns: companies that focus only on
short-term profits versus those that build for long-term value.
He had case studies, frameworks, and plenty of proof that his
methodology worked. But he was tired of the typical "business-in-a-box" approach. (As are so many of us. Sigh.)

"I've heard about parables and think that might be a better
way to share what I've learned," he told me. "How do I turn
my consulting methodology into a story that actually teaches?
And how do I build interest in it while I'm writing?"

Here's what I'd tell Marcus over a gallon or so of coffee.
(Marcus wasn't the type to go for bubble tea.)

Why Parables Work for Business Content

Marcus, you're absolutely right to consider the parable format,
and you're smart to think about audience building while you
write. In the last few years, I've had a number of clients choose
to write parables instead of the usual business-in-a-box drivel.
The results have been remarkable—books like Josh Patrick's
Sustainable and Vicki Suiter's *The Profit Bleed* prove that readers
learn best not from an endless stream of concepts but from
simple stories that don't take seven years to write. Business
parables allow you to discuss complex strategies through concrete narratives that are easily understood and remembered.

The power of parables lies in their ability to position you
as a guide without being preachy. Instead of lecturing about

sustainable growth principles, you show them in action through relatable characters facing real challenges.

Building Your Parable from Existing Material

Looking at your scavenger hunt material, you've got the raw ingredients: client case studies showing the consequences of short-term thinking, success stories from companies that embraced sustainable practices, and your proven methodology for helping businesses transition.

But here's where the rubber meets the road, Marcus. You're not just going to outline your parable—we'll get to outlining during the next step—you're going to write your first story brick right now. Let's take one of your core principles and turn it into an actual scene.

Think about your most dramatic client example of short-term thinking gone wrong. Maybe it's the tech startup that burned through venture capital by scaling too fast, or the retail company that cut customer service to boost quarterly profits and lost their loyal customers. Pick one that still makes you shake your head.

Now, instead of presenting this as a case study, you're going to dramatize it. Let's say your protagonist is David, the CEO of a growing software company. Here's how you'd develop your first parable scene:

Setting the Scene: David sits in his glass-walled conference room, staring at spreadsheets showing declining cash flow. The office beyond buzzes with activity—his team of 50 employees working frantically to meet impossible deadlines. On his desk sits a termination letter for his VP of Customer Success, the person who's been warning him about retention problems for months.

The Critical Moment: Your protagonist faces the decision that will illustrate your principle. Maybe his CFO walks in with two options: lay off 20 employees to meet quarterly projections, or reject a lucrative but unsustainable contract that would overextend the company.

The Wrong Choice: Show David making the short-term decision. Let us hear his internal justification: "We just need to get through this quarter. We'll fix the culture issues later." Give us his body language—the way he avoids eye contact when announcing layoffs, the nervous habit of clicking his pen during the difficult conversation.

The Immediate Consequences: Don't just tell us what happened; show us. The empty desks of laid-off employees. The stressed faces of remaining staff pulling double shifts. The phone call from their biggest client complaining about service quality.

This becomes your opening scene—the "before" picture that sets up your entire parable. You're not just explaining the principle of sustainable growth; you're making readers feel the cost of ignoring it.

Your Next Scenes: Each mini-lesson becomes a chapter where David meets a guide who teaches him one principle. Maybe it's Sarah, the CEO of a competitor who chose long-term thinking during a similar crisis. Show us that conversation—David's skepticism, Sarah's patient explanation, the specific examples she shares of how delayed gratification paid off.

The key is writing actual scenes with dialogue, settings, and character development, not just outlining your business concepts.

The Business Advantage of This Approach

Here's why this works so well for business consultants like you, Marcus: parables make complex business concepts accessible and memorable. Your clients will remember your story long after they've forgotten bullet points from traditional business books. They'll share your story with colleagues, spreading your message organically.

Moreover, business audiences are skeptical of theory without proof. The parable format lets you demonstrate your principles in action rather than just lecture about them.

The Strategic Connection

Crystal and Marcus represent two different applications of the same core strategy: taking your existing expertise and proven results, then wrapping them in compelling stories that make abstract concepts concrete and memorable.

Whether you're writing about spiritual transformation or business principles, your readers need faces to connect with and real situations they can understand. The key is identifying which stories from your scavenger hunt material will best serve your message and your readers' needs.

Crystal's authenticity stories and Marcus's sustainable growth parables aren't just content; they're the emotional center that makes abstract ideas stick. Both writers can test these stories through their existing platforms while developing their books, getting feedback that makes the final manuscript stronger.

Now What? From Story Bricks to Book Structure

You've also seen how these two very different writers applied the brick-building system to their specific projects. You understand how to mine concepts for stories, develop them using story elements, and test them with your audience. You've probably written a few story bricks of your own.

But here's what every writer asks at this point: "I've got all these individual pieces—personal stories, client examples, case studies, concepts I want to explore. How do I turn this pile of content into an actual book that makes sense?"

The answer lies in creating your blueprint—the architectural plan that shows you exactly where each brick belongs. Because while you can build a house with enough bricks and mortar, you need to know where each brick goes to create something that won't fall down.

That's where we're headed next: taking your collection of story bricks and organizing them into a structure that serves your readers and achieves your goals. We're moving from content creation to content organization, from building individual pieces to assembling them into your finished book. Oh, boy!

DO THIS

1. Review your scavenger hunt material looking for the abstract concepts that need concrete illustration—like Crystal's "authenticity" or Marcus's "sustainable growth."

2. Choose your story vehicle: Will you use personal stories, client case studies, or fictional parables to illustrate your points? Base this on your genre requirements and comfort level.

3. Identify the faces your readers will meet. Who are the right guides for your message, and why will your readers connect with them?

4. Connect to your existing content: How can the stories you develop serve double duty as book content and platform material?

5. Test as you build: Share shorter versions of these stories through your platform to see what resonates before committing to full development.

6. Remember: Your stories aren't decoration—they're the vehicles that carry your most important ideas from your expertise into your readers' understanding.

STEP 3

DEVELOPING
AN OUTLINE

9

ORDER IN THE COURT

Use Your Table of Contents to Structure Prescriptive Nonfiction That Readers Actually Want

Not sure where the stories you've just written are going to go? Feeling dangerously disorganized? No worries. There's no one right way to build your book. I repeat: there's no one right way to build your book. An individual story or other type of brick could likely be dropped into fifteen different places throughout your manuscript. More importantly, by the time you complete your last draft, the one that you'll publish, you'll have moved most of your content bits around a dozen times anyway.

Possibilities are great, but for those of you who get a little squirrely without a set plan, we're going to create some structure to keep you cool and composed. We're going to create a blueprint for your book. That way, when you're looking at the magnificent collection of bricks at your feet—whether they're scenes, case studies, research findings, or frameworks—you'll have some idea what to do with them all. You'll know how to organize and connect these seemingly disparate pieces so they come out whole. As Steve Chandler says in his book *Shift Your Mind*, "Energy is robbed by indecision. Not knowing what to do next, trying so hard to decide which course to take, it wears you out." A blueprint will minimize uncertainty, buttress your confidence, and keep you perky enough to march forward.

Your Table of Contents is the first layer of your blueprint, the main organizing schema. The Table of Contents is that page at the very beginning of a book—most books have them, but some don't—that lists the chapter titles and the page numbers on which they begin.

Think a Table of Contents is an afterthought? Something an author slaps together after they've written everything? Think again. Your Table of Contents is first an organizing drawer to make your life easier, then it becomes, with some careful consideration, your sales tool, promise to readers, and roadmap all rolled into one. In our platform-building-while-writing world, it doubles as your market research tool. See how important it is?

A Note to Beautiful Writers

Before we dive in, let's acknowledge that different types of books reveal different things through their tables of content. In fiction, you might see atmospheric chapter titles ("The Night

Everything Changed") or simply numbered chapters, and the Table of Contents mainly shows you pacing and scope. Memoir Tables of Contents reveal whether the author is organizing chronologically, thematically, or around pivotal life moments.

But we're going to focus primarily on prescriptive nonfiction—business books, self-help, expert positioning books, frameworks, and big idea books. Why? Because these are structurally more demanding for beginning authors. Fiction writers can wing it more with intuitive story flow, but prescriptive nonfiction requires careful sequencing of logic, evidence, and reader comprehension. The stakes for getting your organizational structure right are higher when you're trying to teach, persuade, or guide readers through complex concepts. And readers want to see evidence of this in your table of contents.

So, Beautiful Writers, stand down just for a hot minute.

Start with Your Model

The best way to get a feel for organizing content is to turn to the book you chose to model and study the Table of Contents. Take out that book right now—the one you thought would serve as a good model. If you completely disregarded that assignment, lone ranger that you are, choose a prescriptive nonfiction book you have lying around. Or look at one of the book templates found on the Bonus Page, which you can find at www.summitpresspublishers.com/brick. Found the Table of

Contents yet? Good, because I'm going to show you how to use it to create a detailed plan for your book.

When you look at a prescriptive nonfiction Table of Contents, you get a feel for how the entire book is structured. It's your first guide for creating a content placement plan. You can see:

- How an author structures their content. Do they move from simple to complex? Problem to solution? Past to present?
- How many chapters tackle each major concept?
- Where they place their foundational concepts versus advanced material.

This organizational structure becomes your curation framework. Will you move from simple to complex? Will you divide major concepts into multiple chapters? That's the high-level structural decision that determines your chapter order.

> Note: We're not talking about individual content pieces at this moment—what goes into Chapters 2, 3, or 4. That comes later. So hold that thought while I carry on.

From Structure to Reader Engagement

Now that you understand how your Table of Contents serves as your organizational blueprint, we need to talk about what makes readers actually want to follow that blueprint. This is where your chapter titles come in. Your structural organization gets readers from point A to point B logically, but your chapter titles determine whether they're excited enough to make that journey.

Think of it this way: your organizational structure is the skeleton of your book—it ensures everything connects properly and flows in the right sequence. Your chapter titles are the muscle and skin that make that skeleton appealing and irresistible to readers. Both elements work together to create a Table of Contents that not only organizes your content effectively but also sells your book.

Now look at the individual chapter titles in your model book. This is where an author signals tone, makes promises to readers, and creates the curiosity gaps that keep people turning pages. Don't just skim them; really study them. Good titles should practically grab you by the throat.

How Structure and Titles Work Together

Let me show you how structure and titles work together to create reader engagement using James Clear's *Atomic Habits*. Here's what the beginning looks like:

Part I: The Fundamentals

1. The Surprising Power of Atomic Habits
2. How Your Habits Shape Your Identity (and vice versa)
3. How to Build Better Habits in 4 Simple Steps

Part II: The 1st Law – Make It Obvious

1. The Man Who Didn't Look Right

2. The Best Way to Start a New Habit
3. Motivation Is Overrated; Environment Often Matters More
4. The Secret to Self-Control

Notice what's happening here? Clear's structural organization moves from foundational concepts (Part I) to specific implementation strategies (Part II). That's his logical framework—foundation first, then application. But his chapter titles aren't just listing topics; he's making promises. "The Surprising Power," "The Secret to Self-Control," "The Man Who Didn't Look Right." These chapter titles create curiosity gaps that make you want to keep reading while following his carefully planned learning sequence.

Compare that to a generic self-help table of contents that might read:

1. Introduction to Habits
2. Types of Habits
3. How to Change Habits
4. Maintaining New Habits

See the difference? Clear's structure is just as logical, but his titles make you lean in instead of yawn. One creates excitement about following the learning path; the other makes you reach for a double espresso.

What Your TOC Should Signal

Your Table of Contents (TOC)—the combination of your structural organization and your chapter titles—signals your approach to readers. In prescriptive nonfiction, readers have specific expectations:

- **Clear frameworks:** They want to see logical progression and systematic organization.
- **Engaging promises:** Chapter titles should promise specific outcomes that create curiosity.
- **Problem identification and solution presentation:** The structure should move from diagnosis to prescription.

Your chapter titles should promise specific outcomes while your organizational structure demonstrates that you can deliver on those promises systematically.

Speaking of titles that promise specific outcomes, your book title works the same way—it's the ultimate promise that gets readers to pick up your book in the first place. If you want help crafting a book title that grabs attention and clearly communicates your book's value, check out the book title guide on the bonus page at www.summitpresspublishers.com/brick.

Simplicity Wins in Title Creation

For prescriptive nonfiction, the best chapter titles make complex ideas feel accessible. While novels and memoirs allow for more creative, atmospheric titles, business and self-help readers want clarity and direct promises.

Look at what works:

The Five Second Rule by Mel Robbins uses action-oriented titles like "Push Yourself," "Why You Won't Take Action," and "The Tool That Changes Everything"—direct promises that create urgency.

The Life-Changing Magic of Tidying Up chapters focus on specific areas (clothes, books, papers) and specific actions (discard, organize, maintain).

The 7 Habits of Highly Effective People gives you exactly what the title promises—seven distinct, learnable habits.

These examples make promises, create curiosity, and signal clear value without overwhelming complexity. Complexity for the sake of complexity doesn't impress anyone. Clarity does.

Your Blueprint as Business Foundation

Your Table of Contents and chapter structure serve a purpose beyond organizing your book—they become the foundation for building a sustainable business around your expertise. In our platform-building-while-writing world, every chapter you create can work double duty.

Each chapter title and the systematic way you move readers through your content becomes your signature methodology—the distinctive approach that sets you apart from other experts in your field. This organization you establish can scale across multiple platforms:

- **Speaking opportunities:** Each chapter becomes a potential keynote or workshop topic.
- **Content creation:** Chapter themes fuel years of blog posts, newsletters, and social media content.

- **Consulting offerings:** Your systematic approach becomes your service methodology.
- **Course development:** Chapter sequences translate directly into training modules.
- **Thought leadership:** Your unique framework establishes your expertise positioning.

Don't just ask, "Does this chapter order make sense for the book?" Ask, "Can I build a sustainable business around these concepts in this sequence?" The order in which you present your ideas is what makes your approach distinctive and scalable.

Test Before You Build

Before committing to your full blueprint, validate your key concepts with real people. Post your main ideas on social media, propose a talk on your topic, or simply ask your audience what they most want to learn about. This quick validation ensures you're building a blueprint for a book that people actually want to read.

Now that you understand how your Table of Contents serves as your blueprint's foundation, let's put these principles into practice. We're going to start with the most forgiving structure in nonfiction: inspirational books. But first...

DO THIS

1. Study your prescriptive nonfiction model: Locate the Table of Contents in a business, self-help, or framework book. Analyze both the overall structure (how content is organized and sequenced) and the individual chapter titles (what promises they make).

2. Create your promise-making word bank: List ten or more words you might use in chapter titles that signal specific outcomes or create curiosity. Focus on action-oriented and benefit-driven language.

3. Map your structural framework: Based on your model's approach, create a logical progression for your chapters. Will you move from simple to complex? Problem to solution? Foundation to advanced application?

4. Test your chapter titles: Use your potential chapter titles as social media post headlines or newsletter subject lines to see which ones generate the most engagement.

5. Plan your signature methodology: Consider how your chapter sequence could become your distinctive approach that works across speaking topics, workshop modules, and content series.

6. Check your clarity: Make sure each chapter title promises a specific outcome that your target audience actually wants, without overwhelming them with jargon or complexity.

10

SHEILA ON THE EDGE

Turn Your Blog Posts into an Inspirational Book

Why start here with inspirational books? Because if you're a coach, speaker, or consultant who's been creating blog content, you've probably been unconsciously training yourself to write inspirational book chapters without realizing it. Each post likely follows the exact formula that makes these books work: a story or observation, followed by a lesson that readers can apply.

Better yet, inspirational books have a looser set of structural rules than step-by-step guides or business frameworks. While they still need to deliver clear value to readers, they allow more flexibility in how you organize and present your content. This makes them the perfect place to practice blueprint thinking before we tackle more demanding structures.

Let me show you exactly how this works using a real-life example.

Back in the day, one of my students, Sheila, chose to model my husband's inspirational book, *Journeys on the Edge: Living a Life That Matters*. (She was a coach and an expert in her own right, so her choice made a lot of sense.) What made this even more perfect for Sheila was that Walt's book started as a collection of blog posts—just like the content she'd been creating for her own audience.

I happened to have about three hundred copies of Walt's book lying around the house, so I grabbed one of them and got busy.

I'm going to show you how I analyze this book and the Table of Contents to create a blueprint for Sheila. (Notice that I'm bringing us into the present tense to keep things manageable.)

On the back cover of *Journeys*, it says, "Squeezed by time and snared in responsibility, so many of us fail to live the lives we once imagined. But there is another way." From this statement, one can infer that lessons abound.

Analyzing the Structure

Peeking at the Table of Contents, I find a list of forty-two chapters. Again, that's a lot of chapters. This makes sense, however, knowing that this book started out as a collection of blog posts—each post becoming its own short chapter.

Some of these chapter titles are provocative and perhaps a little silly: "The Trouble Newton Caused," "I've Been Framed," and "Before You Know It, It's Lunchtime." This tells me that the book is going to have some humor. I'm curious. What could these titles mean? What might the lessons be? Remember, we want our Table of Contents to hook our readers in this way. When I skim through, I find that each chapter is three or so pages long and ends with a little quote. Just a quick observation.

Walt's introductory chapter is five pages long, and it tells us what the book is about, who the author is, and why we should care about him and his story. He's setting the stage. We know what the struggles will be upfront. Remember, readers want to know what the problem is right away. They don't want to wade through thirty-nine pages or chapters to figure that out. Without a problematic situation, or ten, there's no story. Game over. The book gets tossed.

The Framework Advantage

Heading back to the Table of Contents, I notice that while there are numerous short chapters, they're organized into five sections. These sections are a framework that deserves study.

Section One is called "Resuscitating Your Dreams." It has a subtitle: "Remembering What Rocks Your World." This would imply that all those little chapters housed in this section will have something to do with the broad idea of remembering your dreams. Section Two is called "Eating the Elephant," and the subtitle is "Taking the First Bite." (Hmm. Sound familiar?) I figure the associated chapters will be about taking something big, like building a book, breaking it down into manageable steps, and then taking on the first one. The other three sections indicate that this is a guidebook of sorts, where the steps necessary for living the life of your dreams are spelled out and supported with relevant stories. To end the book, we have an epilogue, which serves as a conclusion, tying the ideas into a neat little bundle.

This five-section framework is Walt's signature system, whether he planned it that way or not.

Just so we're keeping horses in front of carts, know that Walt took his individual blog posts—a whole big pile of them—and moved them around like chess pieces to see which reading order made the most sense. After several configurations, he began to see some common themes in his blogs, which gave him the idea of a structure that would hold them all together. His message—the steps for living the life of your dreams—was born of this structure. The personal journey was organic; the organization of it, however, took some manhandling.

This is the exact process you can use with your own blog content. Print out your best posts, spread them across your dining room table, and start looking for patterns. What themes keep showing up? What progression of ideas would make the most sense for a reader who's never encountered your work before?

For inspirational writers, your "system" might be less about step-by-step instructions and more about a philosophy, an approach to life, or a way of thinking that readers can adopt and adapt to their circumstances.

Now that we've analyzed the overall structure—how Walt organizes his forty-two chapters into five thematic sections—it's time to look more closely at what each individual chapter contains, not just the stage-setting introduction or wrap-up epilogue. We need to understand the specific types of content bricks that make up a chapter and how they're arranged. This chapter-level analysis will show you not just what to include in your chapters, but in what order and balance to arrange those elements.

Walt's Chapter Structure

Let's jump ahead to Chapter 12: "The Other F* Word." What's it made of?

Walt starts with an idea, the F-word. Naughty minxes that we are, we think it means "fuck," but he pulls the old bait and switch and tells us he means "failure." He takes this broad topic—failure—and tells us a short story about what was expected of him in his family of origin and how he wasn't supposed to fail. This is a pencil sketch without a lot of sensory detail; few story elements save character and dialogue. He follows this story with several quotes about failure from other sources; there are six in all. Then we learn about Walt's friend Bob—this could be a client or an acquaintance—who has a very different take on the issue. This is an opportunity to consider failure from a different perspective in more depth. Walt wraps the chapter up by giving us a takeaway, a little lesson that he's learned by looking at failure through these other lenses: "If we don't retreat from failure, but learn from it instead, it can catapult us to brilliance." This is his conclusion, his point.

The other chapters seem to follow this formula: broad idea, supporting stories, and a lesson at the end. Sound familiar?

I knew it would. If you've been blogging consistently, you've probably been using this exact structure without realizing it.

Sound like the kind of book you'd like to write? If you're an expert, a speaker, or a coach with a collection of blog posts, I'm betting the answer is yes.

What do your steps look like? How would you break down your unique process for your reader? What stories do you have to support your recommended line of action?

The Content Mix for Inspirational Books

Now that you understand Walt's formula—broad idea, supporting stories, and a lesson at the end—let's talk about how to balance these elements in your own chapters. Inspirational books have a different content balance than other genres. Here's what readers typically expect:

Personal Stories (60-70%): The heart of your book. These should be specific, detailed experiences that show rather than tell your lessons. Include sensory details, dialogue, and emotional honesty.

Explicit Lessons (20-25%): Unlike memoir, you need to overtly connect your experiences to insights readers can apply. Don't make them guess what you learned.

Universal Connections (10-15%): Help readers see how your specific experiences relate to broader human challenges—fear, change, relationships, purpose, growth.

Gentle Guidance (5-10%): Not step-by-step instructions, but perspective shifts, questions for reflection, or new ways of thinking about common problems.

The key is maintaining the story-driven nature while ensuring readers walk away with something they can use in their lives. You're not just entertaining them; you're helping them see their challenges differently.

Instructions for Sheila's Blueprint

Now, what would I do if I were Sheila? If I wanted to use the structure of *Journeys on the Edge*, let's break the steps down for Sheila using the Table of Contents. Better yet, let's break the steps down for you.

1. **Take out a blank piece of paper and write down the numbers one through seven.** These represent the introduction chapter, the five major sections, and the epilogue, in that order. Leave a lot of space between the numbers one through seven because we're going to pencil in a little more structure.

2. **Write the word "Introduction" by number one.** Beneath that word, list, line by line, the questions that will need to be answered before you move on: What is this book about? Who are you? Why should the reader care? What specific problem are you solving, and what transformation can readers expect if they follow your system?

3. **For Section One, which you'll jot down by the number two, write the following:** "The most important lesson I've learned, or seen others learn, is _____." As a subset of Section One, write the numbers one

through five. These will represent the blog posts or chapters related to this lesson. Each chapter should tell a specific story illustrating this lesson, then explicitly draw out what readers can learn from your experience.

4. **For Section Two, which you'll type by, that's right, the number three, write the following:** "The second most important lesson I've learned, or seen others learn, is _____." Now, do the same exact thing. And do that for each of the following sections, all the way up to Section Five. Make sure each section builds on your transformation journey—you're showing readers how you evolved from one way of thinking to another.

5. **By number seven, write the word "Epilogue" or "Conclusion."** Then, write this question: "What have these things taught me, and why should others care?" Show readers who you've become as a result of these experiences and what's now possible for them if they embrace similar insights.

Consider this a starting structure. By the time you publish your book, the introduction and conclusion will have been revised multiple times. The sections will have shape-shifted because you'll learn that what you thought was the lesson was not really the lesson at all. You're not going to know that, however, until you write the first shitty draft and test it with real people. To get to the final product, you must start. And it's so much easier to start when you can see, in black and white, what you'll need to produce.

DO THIS

1. Using the model book analysis approach from Chapter 9, examine the length and composition of the chapters. Are they filled with quotes, lists, bullet points, research citations, and step-by-step processes? Are the lessons clear? Do the stories support the points?

2. Answer this: How is the unique process broken down for the reader? Is it built into a step-by-step structure that readers can follow systematically?

3. Identify the author's signature framework or system. How could you develop something similar for your area of expertise?

4. If you have existing blog content, gather your best posts and look for patterns. What themes emerge? What natural progression do you see? How might you organize these into sections that tell a larger story about transformation or growth?

5. Consider how you could test each major concept with your audience before writing the whole book. What platforms do you have access to for content testing?

6. Make some notes about what you'll need in your chapters to serve as a guideline, either in your story notebook or in the model book itself. (That's why I told you to buy the thing!)

11

BLUEPRINT BY NUMBERS

The 14-Chapter Template for Prescriptive Nonfiction That Never Fails

nspirational books offer a gentle introduction to blueprint thinking because they grow organically from your existing stories and experiences. But what if your expertise demands more systematic organization? What if you're teaching complex business strategies, step-by-step processes, or comprehensive frameworks that readers need to understand in a specific sequence?

That's where having a proven structural template becomes invaluable.

When Templates Work Best

While there's no single "right" way to organize prescriptive nonfiction, most beginning authors benefit from starting with a tested framework rather than inventing structure from scratch.

Think of the difference this way: Walt's inspirational book emerged organically from his blog posts, like a garden that grows naturally from scattered seeds, the kind that haven't been rotting in a drawer for years on end. (Is that just me?) But if you're teaching marketing systems, productivity frameworks, or business strategies, your readers need a more engineered approach—like building a house where the foundation must come before the walls, and the walls before the roof.

When to Use Templates vs. Organic Structure

Not every book needs a rigid template. Use the organic approach (like we saw with Walt's book) when:

- Your expertise centers around mindset shifts and perspective changes.
- You have strong story-driven content that teaches through example.
- Your "system" is more philosophy than step-by-step process.
- Your blog posts naturally cluster around themes rather than sequential steps.

Use a structural template when:

- You're teaching specific methodologies that build upon each other.
- Your expertise involves complex processes with multiple components.
- Readers need to master foundational concepts before advancing.
- Your content is more instructional than inspirational.

The template approach works particularly well for business books, self-help guides, how-to manuals, and any book where readers expect systematic guidance from problem to solution. If you're not sure which camp you fall into, lean toward the template—it's easier to loosen up a rigid structure than to impose order on chaos

How to Work with Book Templates

Before we dive into the specific 14-chapter structure, let's talk about how to actually use any book template effectively. Understanding how to work with templates will save you loads of time.

What Templates Are (And What They're Not)

Think of your template like an Ina Garten recipe—it tells you what ingredients you need and in what proportions, but you still have to do the actual cooking. Templates are structural guides, not fill-in-the-blank worksheets. They show you what type of content belongs where and how much space to give each element.

Before You Begin: Analyze Your Content Treasure Trove

You've already done the scavenger hunt work from Chapter 5—gathering your existing content, identifying stories both personal and client-related, and starting to see patterns in your material. Now we need to get more systematic about analyzing what you've collected so you can see how these pieces might fit into a template structure.

Time to spread everything out on your dining room table (or kitchen counter, or office floor—wherever you have space to make a proper mess) and really examine what you've got.

Step 1: Gather Everything You've Collected

Pull out all that material you've been accumulating:

- Blog posts and articles
- Social media posts that got significant engagement
- Newsletter content and email sequences
- Presentation slides and speaking notes
- Client worksheets, case studies, and frameworks
- Video/podcast transcripts and course materials
- Stories you tell repeatedly in conversations

Step 2: Sort Your Content by Brick Type

Not all content bricks are created equal. Separate them into these categories:

Story Bricks: Personal experiences that taught you something, client transformation stories, failure stories, "aha moments," origin stories

Teaching Bricks: Step-by-step processes, frameworks, principle explanations, how-to instructions, troubleshooting guides

Proof Bricks: Case studies with results, supporting data/research, before-and-after examples, testimonials, industry examples

Philosophy Bricks: Your beliefs about your field, why traditional approaches fail, your vision for what's possible, mindset shifts

Step 3: Assess Your Brick Quality

Not every piece of content belongs in your book. For each brick, ask:

- Does this serve the book's main transformation promise?
- Is this my best thinking, or have I evolved beyond it?
- Does this fit the tone and depth I want?
- Will this resonate with my ideal reader?

Don't try to cram everything you've ever written into this one project—that way lies madness and reader overwhelm.

Step 4: Map Your Bricks to Template Slots

For each chapter in the template, ask:

- What content do I already have that fits these require-ments?
- What do I need to create to fill the gaps?
- How can I arrange these pieces to best serve my reader?

Don't force content where it doesn't belong naturally. The template works when it helps organize your thinking, not when it becomes a straitjacket for your expertise.

Remember: Templates Are Starting Points

Your expertise and voice matter more than perfect template adherence. Use the structure as a foundation, but adapt it to serve your specific content and reader needs. The goal is creat-ing a clear path through your expertise, not forcing your bril-liance into someone else's box.

Now that you understand how to work with templates and when to use them, let's get to it.

The 14-Chapter Template

Here's a proven structure that works for most prescriptive nonfiction books. Think of this as your blueprint's backbone—you can adjust the specifics, but the underlying framework will keep you on track. (Yes, you'll find other templates on the bonus page, www.summitpresspublishers.com/brick but stick with me while I expound on this one.)

Foundation Chapters (Chapters 1-2): Hook and Overview

These first two chapters do the heavy lifting of getting readers invested in your book. Chapter 1 establishes why you're worth listening to—as opposed to a nattering hyena—and what problem you're solving. Chapter 2 shows your complete system in action so readers can see where you're taking them.

Chapter 1: Expert Positioning & Problem Identification (11-16 pages)

- Personal story that led to your expertise (2-3 pages)
- Clear definition of the problem your system solves
- Who this works for (comprehensive list)
- Why traditional approaches fail

Key Questions to Answer:

- What pivotal moment or story establishes your expertise?
- What's the core problem people face in your field?
- Who specifically is your ideal reader?
- What are the common failed approaches in your industry?

Chapter 2: System Overview with Case Study (11-16 pages)

- Detailed case study (2 pages opening)
- Complete system breakdown using the case study
- Clear step-by-step overview of your method
- What readers can expect from the rest of the book

Key Questions to Answer:

- What's your most compelling transformation story?
- How does your system work from start to finish?
- What are the key phases or steps of your methodology?
- What results can readers realistically expect?

Core Teaching Chapters (Chapters 3-5): Foundation Principles

Now you're getting into the meat of your expertise. These three chapters teach the fundamental concepts that everything else builds on. If readers only absorbed these chapters, they should still walk away with significant value from your book.

Chapter 3: Foundation Principle #1 (11-16 pages)

- Personal discovery story (2 pages)
- Why this principle is essential
- How it connects to your case study from Chapter 2
- Proof or data supporting this principle

Key Questions to Answer:

- What story illustrates why this principle matters?
- What happens when people ignore this principle?
- How does this principle work in practice?
- What proof can you provide of its effectiveness?

Chapter 4: Foundation Principle #2 (11–16 pages)

- Personal discovery moment
- Clear definition of the concept
- Extended case study showing application
- Practical implementation guidance

Key Questions to Answer:

- How did you discover this principle?
- What exactly is this concept and why does it work?
- What's a detailed example of someone using this successfully?
- How can readers implement this immediately?

Chapter 5: Core Methodology Deep Dive (11–16 pages)

- Historical context of your method
- Detailed teaching of core content
- Essential elements readers must know
- Bridge to implementation chapters

Key Questions to Answer:

- How did you develop this methodology?
- What are the non-negotiable elements of your system?
- What common mistakes do people make when learning this?
- How does this set up the implementation phase?

Implementation Chapters (Chapters 6–8): Making It Work

This is where readers roll up their sleeves and get their little hands dirty. These chapters are practical, tactical, and focused on helping people actually do the work. Less philosophy, more step-by-step guidance.

Chapter 6: Implementation Strategy #1 (11–16 pages)

- Direct instruction (no story opening)
- Step-by-step implementation guide
- Example copy/templates
- Visual aids and decision trees

Key Questions to Answer:

- What are the specific steps to implement this?
- What does good execution look like?
- What templates/examples can you provide?
- What are the key decision points in this process?

Chapter 7: Implementation Strategy #2 (11–16 pages)

- Case study opening (3 pages)
- Primary instruction on this phase
- Common obstacles and solutions
- Connection to next implementation phase

Key Questions to Answer:

- What case study best illustrates this phase?
- What are the key activities in this implementation phase?
- What typically goes wrong and how do you fix it?
- How does this connect to what's coming next?

Chapter 8: Implementation Strategy #3 (11–16 pages)

- Case study with specific results
- Advanced tactical guidance
- Example copy/materials
- Troubleshooting guide

Key Questions to Answer:

- What advanced case study proves this works?
- What are the sophisticated tactics in this phase?
- What examples can you show of excellent execution?
- How do you handle the most common problems?

Advanced Chapters (Chapters 9–11): Scaling and Growth

Readers who've mastered the basics are ready for more sophisticated strategies. These chapters separate your system from beginner-level advice and position you as someone who understands advanced applications.

Chapter 9: Advanced Strategy #1 (11–16 pages)

- Case study opening (2-3 pages)
- Teaching of advanced concept
- When to use this strategy vs. basics
- Integration with previous chapters

Key Questions to Answer:

- What case study shows this advanced strategy?
- How does this strategy work for scaling/growth?
- Who should use this advanced approach?
- How does this build on earlier concepts?

Chapter 10: Advanced Strategy #2 (11–16 pages)

- Personal story leading to lesson (3 pages)
- Advanced strategy instruction
- ROI/results expectations
- Preparation for business applications

Key Questions to Answer:

- What personal experience taught you this strategy?
- How does this advanced method work?
- What kind of results should people expect?
- How does this prepare them for bigger opportunities?

Chapter 11: Business Model/Scaling Formula (11-16 pages)

- Case study opening (3 pages)
- Connection to previous case studies
- Key principles for business building
- Evolution from method to business

Key Questions to Answer:

- What case study shows business transformation?
- How do previous examples connect to business building?
- What are the essential principles for scaling?
- How does someone evolve from practitioner to business owner?

Integration Chapters (Chapters 12-14): Lifestyle and Next Steps

The final stretch brings everything together and sends readers off with inspiration, ongoing guidance, and ways to stay connected to your work.

Chapter 12: Essential Success Principles (11-16 pages)

- Success fundamentals that support your method
- Mindset and habit formation
- Community and support needs
- Long-term sustainability

Key Questions to Answer:

- What fundamentals do readers need for long-term success?
- What mindset shifts are essential?
- Why is community/support important?
- How do people maintain momentum over time?

Chapter 13: Philosophy & Lifestyle Integration (11-16 pages)

- Personal story and history
- Life philosophy and broader vision
- How your method transforms lives beyond the obvious results
- Inspiration and possibility

Key Questions to Answer:

- What's your personal philosophy about this work?
- How has your method transformed your own life?
- What kind of life can readers create?

- What does success look like beyond the obvious metrics?

Chapter 14: Next Steps & Continued Growth (6–8 pages)

- Reiteration of why your system works
- Implementation timeline and expectations
- Resources for continued learning
- How to stay connected

Key Questions to Answer:

- Why should readers trust your system?
- What should they expect as they implement?
- What additional resources will support their journey?
- What's the natural next step for serious students?

Mapping Your Content to the Template

Now that you see the structure, here's how to match your content to the template:

Foundation Chapters (1–2):

- Which story bricks establish your expertise and credibility?
- What proof bricks demonstrate the problem your system solves?
- Which case study bricks show your complete system in action?

Core Teaching Chapters (3-5):

- Which teaching bricks explain your fundamental principles?
- What story bricks illustrate how you discovered these principles?
- Which proof bricks validate each core concept?

Implementation Chapters (6-8):

- Which teaching bricks provide step-by-step guidance?
- What proof bricks show successful implementation?
- Which story bricks reveal common implementation challenges?

Advanced Chapters (9-11):

- Which teaching bricks cover sophisticated strategies?
- What proof bricks demonstrate scaling and advanced results?
- Which story bricks show business transformation?

Integration Chapters (12-14):

- Which philosophy bricks explain your worldview?
- What story bricks show lifestyle and mindset integration?
- Which teaching bricks provide ongoing guidance?

After mapping your bricks, you'll see three types of gaps:

Missing Bricks: Template slots with no existing content. These represent new content you need to create.

Incomplete Bricks: Content that covers part of what a chapter needs but requires additional material. For example, you might have the teaching brick but need a story brick to illustrate the concept.

Loose Bricks: Great content that doesn't fit your current template structure. Don't force these bricks where they don't belong—save them for future projects or bonus materials.

Okay, let's come back to treating templates with respect, not assuming it will work for your content regardless of what you've got. This is not a get-out-of-jail-free card; it's a tool. Use it accordingly.

Template Flexibility and Limitations

When to Modify the Template:

- If your system has fewer than three core principles, combine Chapters 3-5
- If your implementation is simpler, reduce Chapters 6-8 to two chapters
- If you're not teaching business scaling, replace Chapters 9-11 with additional case studies or applications

When the Template Won't Work:

- If your expertise is primarily story-driven rather than system-driven

- If you're sharing a personal journey rather than teaching methodology
- If your content doesn't follow a logical progression from basic to advanced

Content Balance Formula:

As you fill in your template, aim for:

- **40% Teaching/Instruction:** Your core methodology and how-to content
- **30% Stories/Case Studies:** Proof points and reader engagement
- **20% Implementation:** Practical application and examples
- **10% Philosophy/Vision:** Inspiration and bigger picture thinking

Your Blueprint Worksheet

Time to put this baby to work:

1. **Write your book's core transformation:** What specific change will readers experience?
2. **Identify your signature methodology:** What's your unique system or approach?
3. **List your proof stories:** What case studies and personal stories demonstrate your expertise?
4. **Define your ideal reader:** Who exactly needs this information?
5. **Map your 14 chapters:** Using the template above, write chapter titles that reflect your specific content.

6. **For each chapter, answer the key questions** provided in the template.

7. **Create your content outline:** Under each chapter title, list:

- The main teaching point.
- The supporting story or case study.
- The implementation guidance.
- The transition to the next chapter.

Reality Check Questions

Before you get all starry-eyed about your brilliant blueprint, ask yourself:

1. Does this book establish the expertise you want to be known for?

2. Can you create ongoing content around these themes for two to three years?

3. Do you know exactly who will read this book and why they'll care?

4. What specific transformation will engaged readers experience?

5. How is your approach different from other books on similar topics?

6. Do you have ways to reach your ideal readers?

You now have something most would-be authors never get—a complete outline that shows you exactly what you're building and why readers will want it. You know what content bricks you already possess, what you still need to create, and where each piece fits in your structure. More importantly, you've created a Table of Contents that promises readers something specific and valuable, something you're uniquely qualified to deliver. No more staring at blank pages wondering what comes next. No more second-guessing whether your book idea has merit. You have a roadmap that leads from your expertise to your readers' transformation. Now it's time to start building.

DO THIS

1. Complete your content audit using the steps outlined above (if you skipped gathering your content in Chapter 5, shame on you—go back and do it).
2. Choose one successful book in your genre to study alongside this template.
3. Create your 14-chapter outline using the template structure.
4. Answer the key questions for each chapter.
5. Write a one-paragraph description of what each chapter will accomplish.
6. Create your content inventory chart to see what you have and what you need.

12

TUESDAYS WITH MAGGIE

Create a Structure for Your Memoir

The 14-chapter template works beautifully for systematic expertise—but what if your story doesn't fit into neat problem-solution frameworks? What if you're not teaching a methodology but sharing a journey that transformed you?

That's where we enter the messier, more intuitive territory of memoir. If prescriptive nonfiction is like building with precision-engineered components, memoir is like sculpting with clay—messier, more personal, requiring different tools entirely.

Memoir resists rigid templates because every life story is unique. But that doesn't mean memoir lacks structure. The best memoirs follow recognizable patterns that you can analyze and adapt, just like we did with prescriptive books. The difference? Instead of organizing around problems and solutions, memoir organizes around transformation and meaning.

Let me show you exactly how this works using one of my students as an example.

Maggie's Memoir Obsession

One of my early students—I'll call her Maggie—decided she wanted to write a book like *Tuesdays with Morrie*. Confident in her writing skills, she felt ready to take on an involved memoir. More than anything, she yearned to tell the story of her mentors and how they influenced the woman she'd become.

Have you chosen to write a memoir, too, even though I tried to scare you off? Well, listen up; this chapter is just for you. If you're writing a novel or even an inspirational book, you'll find some excellent points here, as well.

Using Maggie's example, let's get to work on creating a blueprint. I'll show you, step by step, how I analyze both the Table of Contents and the book itself to create a replicable structure that works.

Tuesdays with Morrie in All Its Glory

According to the cover of *Tuesdays with Morrie*, this memoir is about an old man, a young man, and life's greatest lesson. Published in 1997, it was enormously popular in the States. I remember it well; perhaps you do too—particularly if you're receiving literature from AARP. It had heart.

This book is a perfect teaching tool because it clearly demonstrates memoir structure and the integration of personal story with universal themes. The lessons emerge naturally from the relationships and conversations, which is exactly how good memoir should work—then and now.

Sure, the memoir landscape has evolved since 1997. Today's successful memoirs often blend personal narrative with broader insights, and many authors use their books to establish expertise and build platforms. However, the fundamental structure that makes *Tuesdays with Morrie* work—the combination of intimate relationship, universal themes, and clear transformation—remains the gold standard for memoir.

Consider what draws a massive readership in today's market:

- *Educated* by Tara Westover: A personal story about family and education that resonates with themes of self-determination and transformation.
- *Becoming* by Michelle Obama: A personal journey that connects with readers interested in leadership, authenticity, and overcoming obstacles.
- *Kitchen Confidential* by Anthony Bourdain: Behind-the-scenes stories that offer insights into an industry and a life philosophy.

Each of these follows the same pattern as *Tuesdays with Morrie*: deeply personal story + universal themes + clear transformation = compelling memoir. The delivery might be different, but the blueprint is remarkably consistent.

Dissecting the Structure

Opening the Table of Contents of *Tuesdays with Morrie*, I see a list of twenty-seven chapters. That's a lot of chapters, but many are very short—only one or two pages long. The others run about seven pages. This gives me a feel for the book's pacing. Short chapters offer a quick read, which busy readers appreciate. (See how you can learn so much from a simple Table of Contents?)

Here are some chapter titles: "The Curriculum," "The Syllabus," "The Student." These are all academic words that establish the theme right away. I'm going to expect a tale about a college-style relationship, one involving higher learning.

Then I find a different type of chapter title: "The 1st Tuesday." This has a subtitle that serves as a description: "We Talk About the World."

This is followed by "The 2nd Tuesday: We Talk About Feeling Sorry for Yourself."

We get all the way to "The Fourteenth Tuesday: We Say Good-Bye" and then have "Conclusion."

The lessons are clearly spelled out in the subtitles. I know exactly what I'll be getting from this book.

Does this structure—lesson embedded in story—sound familiar? It should. It's the same formula we saw in Walt's inspirational book, just applied to a more personal, relationship-driven narrative.

What's Inside Each Chapter

If I were Maggie, I'd take a closer look at these chapters to see what they're composed of. The first chapter is little more than a single page—an introduction telling us in simple yet emotional terms what this story is about. Nothing fancy.

There's a page break that transports the reader from the present moment back in time. We get another page and a half of backstory, where we witness the young man graduating from college and introducing his parents to Morrie. The old man is crying because their relationship means something beyond what one would expect. This backstory is in italics—the author's way of clarifying the time jump.

The first few chapters bring the reader into the story and give us the faces. They answer the crucial questions:

1. Who do we have here?
2. Why should I care about these people?
3. How do they feel about each other?
4. What's at stake for them—what do they stand to lose?
5. Why should I want to know more about them and their situation?
6. What can I learn from their experience that will help me in my own life?

This sixth question is crucial. Readers want to be entertained, yes, but they also want to be transformed. Your memoir needs to offer both.

Let's jump to "The 4th Tuesday: We Talk About Death." We start immediately with a scene: the two men talking in a home office. The lesson about dying is right up front in the dialogue: "Let's begin with this idea," Morrie said. "Everyone knows they're going to die, but nobody believes it."

Notice that the lesson is embedded in the dialogue, not spelled out separately like it would be in a business book. In memoir, we need the lessons tucked into the story. They can't be too obvious, or you score a D- for being pedantic.

What else do we have besides this conversation? We see the backyard through the window, which places us deeper in the setting. We get details about what's happening in Detroit, where the young man lives, grounding us in that era. We're given snippets of each man's current life, philosophy, and personal history woven through this conversation, which resembles a truly powerful college lecture.

The Timeless Memoir Formula

Having flipped through the remaining chapters, I can see what this book really is: a collection of stories about death and what someone who is dying can teach us about living. Spelled out in twenty-seven short chapters are the lessons and the story of the relationship, which is the book's emotional heart. We care about the message because we care about the faces.

This formula works as well today as it did in 1997:

- **Compelling relationship** (the emotional hook)
- **Universal themes** (what everyone can relate to)
- **Clear lessons** (what readers can apply)
- **Visible transformation** (how the narrator changes)

Modern memoir writers might add platform-building elements or position themselves as experts, but they're building on this same foundation. The core structure remains solid.

The Memoir Content Mix

Unlike prescriptive nonfiction, memoir has its own content balance requirements. Here's what successful memoirs typically contain:

Scenes and Dialogue (70-80%): The heart of your memoir. These should be specific, detailed moments that show rather than tell your story. Remember those story elements from Chapter 6? This is where you use them—setting, character, plot, dialogue, and sensory details to recreate experiences for your reader.

Reflection and Meaning-Making (15-20%): Your insights about what these experiences meant, how they changed you, and what readers can learn. Unlike business books, these lessons should feel discovered, not preached.

Context and Background (5-10%): Just enough explanation to help readers understand the setting, timeframe, and circumstances. Don't bog down your scenes with excessive backstory.

The key is leaning heavily toward showing rather than telling. Most failed memoirs spend too much time explaining and not enough time letting readers experience the story alongside you.

Instructions for Maggie's Blueprint

Now, what the hell is Maggie supposed to do with this analysis? Maybe you don't care about Maggie, being selfish and all, but you'd probably like to know how this applies to you.

Maggie is going to sketch a blueprint for her book using the *Tuesdays with Morrie* structure:

1. **Break out a piece of paper and number one through sixteen** from top to bottom, representing your chapters. Why not twenty-seven like the original? That's too complicated to start with, so I'm giving you a shortcut.

2. **Chapter one will be your introduction.** Mitch Albom broke his introduction into five short chapters. For simplicity's sake, you're going to do it in one. Answer these questions: Who are these people, and what is this story about? What transformation will readers witness, and what can they learn from it? If readers don't know this upfront, they won't press on.

3. **Chapters two through fifteen will be your lessons.** Here's where memoir gets tricky. If you don't know why you're writing about these people and what those fourteen lessons were, you need to stop and do some soul-searching. Each lesson should emerge from experiences you can ethically and accurately recreate—meaning you remember enough detail to build compelling scenes, and sharing these stories won't destroy relationships or violate others' privacy.

   Ask yourself for each potential lesson: What universal human experience does this specific story illuminate? If you can't answer that clearly, it's not ready for your book. Remember, just because something significant happened to you doesn't mean strangers will care. Your lessons need to serve readers, not just help you process your experiences.

4. **Chapter sixteen will be your conclusion.** What do you make of all these lessons when all is said and done? What do you understand about life now that you didn't before? How has this knowledge changed you? Without visible transformation, we've got nothing worth writing about or reading. And if you're building a platform, how are you using these insights to help others?

As you develop your blueprint, keep in mind that memoir involves real people who didn't sign up to be in your book. You'll need to change names and identifying details when necessary, and some stories might be better left untold—at least for now. Focus on emotional truth over factual precision, especially when memory gets fuzzier than a peach about specific details from years past.

Let's Get Real, Memoir Writers

Before you dive into your blueprint, be honest about your goals. Are you writing primarily for yourself, your family, and close friends? Or do you want to reach a broader audience and potentially build a platform around your story?

There's no wrong answer, but the approach differs. If you're writing for personal reasons, focus on telling your story authentically. The blueprint still helps with organization, but you don't need to worry about universal appeal.

If you want to reach a broader audience like Maggie does, think strategically about how your personal story connects with themes that resonate widely. Your memoir becomes both a personal narrative and a professional positioning tool.

A Final Note

Do this, do that, but don't do this.... It's easy to forget that your story matters, that your journey can light the way for someone else's transformation. But the blueprint you'll be creating just ensures that your important story gets told in a way that readers can follow, understand, and use.

Stop overthinking it and start building that blueprint. Your story is waiting.

And yet... here's where things get interesting: having a solid structure doesn't magically make the writing easy. Lord, I wish it did. In fact, now that you can see the full scope of what you need to write, you might be feeling a little overwhelmed. Don't panic. Every writer hits obstacles, and memoir writers face some unique challenges we haven't talked about yet. That's what Step 4 is all about—staying steady when the writing gets tough.

DO THIS

1. Study your chosen memoir model using the approach we used with *Tuesdays with Morrie*. Examine chapter length, composition, and the balance between scene and reflection.

2. Track the time structure: How does the author handle chronology? Do they move linearly through time or jump between past and present? Note how they signal time shifts.

3. Identify the relationship at the center: What's the key relationship that drives the story? Why do we care about these people and their connection?

4. Map the transformation arc: What version of the author do we meet at the beginning versus the end? Identify three to five key moments that show this change.

5. List your fourteen lessons: What universal insights emerge from your specific experience? Each lesson becomes a chapter in your blueprint.

6. Test your memoir concept: Can you explain in one sentence what your book is about and why someone who doesn't know you would want to read it? If not, keep refining until you can.

7. If your memoir involves complex family dynamics or cultural elements, check out the detailed *Educated* template on the bonus page at www.summitpresspublishers.com/brick. Some stories need more sophisticated structural approaches than the *Tuesdays with Morrie model.*

STEP 4

STAYING STEADY THROUGH THE STORM

13

THERE WILL BE OBSTACLES AND BLOOD

Overcome Fear, Doubt, and Every Other Writing Saboteur

'm going to assume that you've been doing exactly what I've told you to do because you're either compliant or very keen on finishing your book. If you've been writing up a storm, you've likely run into some obstacles. Everyone does. You may be pacing back and forth, chewing your nails, because you have no idea what to do next. How, pray tell, are you going to push ahead with that glaring problem staring you in the face?

Yes, your job right now is to create a shitty first draft. Yes, your job is to gather and make as many bricks—stories, concepts, frameworks—as you can. And yes, you have a good idea of where your bricks should eventually go, given your genre and the outcome you're after. Maybe even a handy dandy template. But some issues feel like showstoppers. When you sit down to write, you actually feel afraid.

I bet you're thinking something is wrong with you, with the way you're doing things, because you've forgotten that a good writer can make it all look so damn easy. Look at James Clear with *Atomic Habits*—his concepts seem so simple and clear. Consider Brené Brown, who makes vulnerability and shame research sound like a casual dinner conversation she just tossed onto the page. Zero effort required.

Well, well, well... Here's what you don't see: James Clear spent years testing his ideas through his newsletter, refining concepts through thousands of reader interactions before writing his book and getting all the words right. Brené Brown gave hundreds of presentations, failed at several book proposals, and wrestled with academic writing conventions before finding her voice (and probably her framework).

The polished final product is never the whole story. When you see their success, you're seeing the end result of years of work, false starts, and refinement. As God is my witness, doubt *will* set in like a bugger if you compare your shitty first draft to their polished final product.

Welcome to writing.

Dry your tears, my pet. In this section, we're going to address some of the most common issues and fears that crop up along the way—including some new ones that didn't exist when writers could hide in their garrets and emerge, all blinky-eyed, clutching their completed masterpieces.

The Trouble with Beavers

But before I begin, I'm going to make a point: When you run into an obstacle, any obstacle, do not run away from it. Don't start a different story (or even a different project) thinking it will be easier because you don't immediately know how to solve your problem. Be patient.

Now, I'm going to tell you a story: Long, long ago, my husband, Walt, and I were out for a morning run. Our running route took us past a river, and being springtime, we began to notice signs of increased animal activity. The beavers, in particular, had been very busy.

We trotted past an enormous oak tree. The beavers had been gnawing on it for weeks, and they were close to bringing the whole tree down. Another day or so of work, and the trunk would likely snap in half. A little farther down the road, I noticed that the beavers had started in on another tree. They'd done quite a job on it as well. That's when I spotted the rest. I counted all the partially gnawed trees, and do you know how many there were? Fifteen! Not a single one had been taken down, which, I believe, is the beaver's goal.

For those unfamiliar with the habits of North American wildlife, a beaver's job is to bring trees down into the water to construct a dam. They live in small, calm pools created by these dams. Dams don't miraculously appear because a beaver would like them to; they must be built. That's how nature works.

Being the intuitive sort, I could practically hear what these beavers were thinking. "Damn, I'm tired. I don't know how much longer I've got to chew on this stupid tree." Leaning back on its tail and looking around, one of them must have spied a smaller tree, a tree with deceptively soft bark. "Let's go for that one. That one looks easier to take down. Not as big, not so complicated."

You might not know this, but beavers are short and quite near-sighted. They can't step back far enough to see the trees for the forest. They're blind to the fact that if they just kept at it, if they just worked through the ubiquitous obstacles, that old oak would fall sooner rather than later. Cursed with poor memories as well, beavers are also incapable of remembering that the minute they start in on a different tree, they will, as God is their witness, invariably run into the same set of problems they encountered with the first.

Don't be a beaver.

Stick with your big tree and gnaw on it until you take the damn thing down. Your job is to get that tree in the water, not to chew on fifteen different trunks. Trust that, like a nearly blind beaver, you don't have a decent vantage point. You can't tell how long your project is going to take until it's done, and that's okay. Be patient. Keep gnawing. Don't quit and scurry off to work on something that looks easier. Adjust your angle, brush your teeth—whatever it takes—just keep at it.

Too Much of a Good Thing

On a related topic, if you're just getting started, having too many ideas to choose from may not sound like much of a problem. I mean, complaining about your active imagination and your endless downloads from the Universe is not unlike whining about your inability to gain weight. You'd be hard-pressed to find people to feel sorry for you. But what if you have so many ideas you can't home in on a clear direction? What do you do when you're all over the place? When you want to write fifteen different stories, create three different LinkedIn posts to gauge interest, and tackle five different book projects all at once?

Ohhhhh, this problem has gotten so much worse, by the way, what with social media constantly feeding us new ideas and the pressure to create content for platform building. You could write this, share that, and bounce off that great idea you somehow never thought of. But the solution remains the same: pull out your outline. Focus on the outline. Don't run off into Creative Land half-cocked.

There's a good reason I asked you to create an outline for yourself. Yes, this outline will likely change by the time your book is done, but for now, it serves as an organizational tool and a filter for all those shiny ideas.

Got a brilliant story idea? Terrific! Write it down in your story notebook: *I want to write about my client, Gertrude. I want to mention her fear of cats, how she's been married twelve times, and how she finally learned to meditate and lose 300 pounds.* Write until you can't think of another idea. Write until you exhaust your mania.

Then, go back to your outline. Where might this story about Gertrude fit? Chapter 2, subsection 4: How to Lose Weight by Meditating? Perfect—develop that story for that chapter. Consider creating a LinkedIn post to gauge interest. Maybe it doesn't fit anywhere in your current book. Perhaps you want to save that insight about surviving divorce for Book Two. Write it down in your story notebook with enough detail so you'll remember what you were thinking in six months.

The key is having a filter. Your book outline becomes the lens through which you evaluate all those brilliant ideas. Does this serve my current book? If yes, develop it. If not, put it in the parking lot for later.

You don't have to deal with everything all at once. That's why you have a story notebook and an outline—so you can decide which stories to focus on first.

The Comparison Trap and Perfectionism (The Social Media Double Whammy)

Here's a newer obstacle that combines two destructive forces: the constant exposure to other people's success stories and the perfectionist need to measure up. LinkedIn is full of posts about six-figure book launches. Instagram showcases bestselling authors at glamorous events. Twitter celebrates seven-figure publishing deals and sold-out speaking gigs. (Even Jane Austen would feel like a failure comparing herself to that!)

This creates a nightmare on Elm Street for perfectionists. Not only do you need your book to be perfect, but it also needs to achieve the kind of "instant" success you see others celebrating online. And here's what Perfectionism whispers: "If you can't guarantee this level of success, why bother writing at all?" Come to think of it, you'll probably need a new wardrobe and your teeth straightened if you're going to pull off the whole successful author thing. You're going to need some time to research that!

We talked about this in chapter 4, but you've been in the game long enough that it bears repeating: those highlight reels you see represent maybe 1% of the actual writing experience.

For every "overnight success" story you come across, there are hundreds of authors grinding through revisions, facing rejection, and wondering if their book will ever see the light of day. You probably walk past them each time you visit a Starbucks, sitting at that communal table with their laptops, nursing their umpteenth latte of the morning.

Perfectionism, man, does you zero good, despite what you may believe.

Brené Brown wrote brilliantly about this in *The Gifts of Imperfection*: "Perfectionism is not self-improvement. Perfectionism is, at its core, about trying to earn approval and acceptance. When failure is not an option, we can forget about learning, creativity, and innovation." And book writing? That requires all of the above.

So, in the interest of getting you out of the comparison trap, unfollow accounts that make you feel inadequate. Limit social media consumption during writing time. Concentrating is hard enough without all those influencer reels. (Gah! Those adorable, domesticated raccoons eating grapes!) Remember that everyone's timeline is different. Your job is to write your book, not to match someone else's definition of success.

Most importantly, stop trying to write the perfect book. That's so boring. Readers don't want perfection—they want connection. They want to see themselves in your struggles, learn from your insights, and feel less alone in their challenges. Imperfect books that help people beat perfect books that intimidate people every single time.

And if social media comparison wasn't enough to paralyze modern writers, technology has thrown us another curveball that's got people questioning whether there's any point in writing at all.

The AI Anxiety

Here's an obstacle that didn't exist when I first wrote this book: anxiety about artificial intelligence replacing writers. You may be wondering if there's any point in learning to write when AI can generate content in seconds. Maybe you're paralyzed by the thought that your book will be competing with AI's breadth and depth, given that it's pulling from boundless resources.

Let me ease your mind: AI can generate content, but it can't generate wisdom, experience, or an authentic voice. It can't share your specific insights from twenty years in your industry. It can't tell your stories or connect your unique dots.

AI for Book Building —A Dose of Reality

By now you've seen me mention AI several times in this book. Rather than leave you piecing together my thoughts, here's your comprehensive guide to what AI can and cannot do for your book project.

The Reality Check First

AI cannot write your book. Period. It can't replicate your decades of industry experience, your specific client stories, or that "aha" moment you had at 2 AM when you cracked the code on something your field has struggled with for years.

Your book's value comes from your scars, failures, and breakthrough moments. AI cannot replicate that authentic voice that makes readers say, "This person gets it."

What AI Cannot Do (No Matter What the Marketing Says)

Replace Your Unique Perspective: AI pulls from existing content across the internet. It cannot generate original insights from your specific experience.

Write Compelling Stories: Your client case studies, your personal failures, your breakthrough moments—these require human judgment about what details matter and what emotions to evoke.

Make Strategic Decisions: Should this chapter come before that one? Is this example too revealing? Will this advice actually help readers? These require human judgment.

Understand Your Audience: AI doesn't know your newsletter subscribers, speaking audience, or ideal clients. It can't gauge what will resonate with your specific readers.

Create Authentic Voice: AI writes in a bland, inoffensive style designed to appeal to everyone and connect with no one. Your voice—with its quirks, opinions, and personality—is what makes readers care.

What AI Actually Excels At

Consistency Checking: For long manuscripts, AI can track character names (yes, even in business books you have "characters"), catch timeline errors, and spot continuity issues.

Research and Fact-Checking: AI can quickly gather background information, verify dates and statistics, and help you find supporting evidence for your arguments. Think of it as a research assistant who never sleeps but always needs fact-checking.

Overcoming Blank Page Syndrome: Stuck staring at a cursor? Ask AI to generate three different opening paragraphs for a chapter. You'll probably hate all of them, but they'll spark ideas for what you actually want to say.

Content Organization: AI can help restructure existing content, suggest chapter reordering, or identify sections that feel out of place. It's surprisingly good at seeing structural patterns you might miss.

First Draft Generation for Basic Sections: Need a straightforward explanation of a process or concept? AI can create a first draft that you then rewrite in your voice. Key word: rewrite.

Language Polish: AI spots repetitive phrases, suggests stronger word choices, and helps vary sentence structure. It's like having a grammar-obsessed intern who works for free.

The Smart Writer's AI Workflow

1. Use AI for research and brainstorming when you're stuck or need background information
2. Let AI create terrible first drafts of basic explanatory content that you then completely rewrite
3. Run your human-written content through AI for grammar checking and consistency review

4. Ask AI to read from your target audience's perspective to identify confusing sections

5. Trust your instincts about which AI suggestions to implement or ignore

Tools Worth Trying

For Grammar and Style: Grammarly, ProWritingAid, or built-in AI features in Word

For Research and Brainstorming: ChatGPT, Claude, or Google's Bard

For Content Analysis: Most AI tools can analyze your existing content for patterns and issues

Budget: Most useful AI tools cost $10-20/month during your writing phase. That's less than one dinner out for a tool that works 24/7.

Smart authors use AI as a tool, not a replacement. As I said, it's excellent for research, brainstorming, and polishing—tasks that support your creative process without replacing your expertise and voice.

Use AI to handle the mechanical stuff so you can focus on what only you can provide: your unique insights, authentic voice, and hard-won wisdom that readers actually want.

AI strengthens the case for experienced, authentic voices rather than weakening it. In a world of generic content, your specific expertise and perspective become even more valuable.

Don't let AI anxiety stop you from writing, but don't let AI promises convince you that writing is now effortless.

Your voice matters. Your experience matters. AI just helps you express both more efficiently.

But let's move on to the next issue that's bound to crop up...

Lose Friends and Alienate People

Writers worry a lot. Worry feeds our procrastination; it's why we'd rather clean that disgusting barbecue grill than sit in front of our computers. We worry that we're hacks, that we have nothing new to say, and that we're wasting time on yet another project we'll never complete. However, there's one fear that looms above them all: the fear of writing about other people and the trouble it may cause.

For professionals writing business books, this often manifests as: *What if I write about real clients without their permission? What if I discuss specific situations that might identify people? What if my case studies betray confidentiality?*

Here's the scoop: As writers, we strive to stay as close to the truth as possible, but we can disguise identities while remaining true to the storyline. Protecting privacy is often as simple as changing names, genders, industries, and a few key details. Don't assume that to get to the heart of the story, you have to expose others.

There are several ways to navigate this. Use disclaimers—check any copyright page, and you're likely to find one. Most business books include language such as: "To protect privacy, names and identifying details have been changed in the case studies presented." You can also place names in quotes to indicate pseudonyms or combine multiple client situations into composite examples.

The memoir problem is trickier. It's hard to camouflage key players in your life story. You can change his name to "Bob" and put him in cowboy boots, but we all know you're describing your alcoholic father or that brother who ended up in prison. Rare is the family member who will take kindly to your version of the truth.

That said, Anne Lamott once joked: "If people wanted you to write warmly about them, they should've behaved better."

Now, here's the practical advice: tell the truth, do so with love and compassion, and accept that some people may not be happy with your perspective.

While you write, protect yourself by keeping your manuscript private. Don't ask family members for feedback during the vulnerable first draft stage. This is the quickest way to shut yourself down.

Information Overload

Finally, let's talk about an obstacle that's exponentially worse than it was in 2014: information overload. You can find a course, a book, a podcast, a YouTube video, or a blog post about any aspect of writing or publishing. In fact, you can probably find hundreds of them. The problem isn't a lack of information; it's an excess of it.

You can spend months researching the perfect writing process, the best publishing path, and the ideal marketing strategy. I know plenty of wannabe authors who do. Meanwhile, your book remains unwritten—a concept you drone on about at cocktail parties. (Yes, this is why those invitations seem to have gotten lost in the mail.)

Here's the antidote: Choose one source of advice (like this book), follow it completely, then evaluate. Don't try to synthesize fifteen different approaches. Don't switch methods every time you read something new.

Most writing advice is sound. The challenge lies not in finding the perfect method but in sticking with one method long enough to see results.

Stop researching. Start writing. You can always course-correct later, but you can't edit a blank page.

Making Your Book Real

Now that we've talked about all the ways you can sabotage yourself, let's focus on something that will help you push through these obstacles: make your book feel real.

One reason writers get derailed by fears and distractions is that their book feels like a vague concept floating in their heads. It's easy to abandon something that doesn't feel concrete. But when your book has a name and becomes a specific project with its own identity, it's much harder to give up on.

Think about it: You're more likely to stick with *The Confidence Code: How to Stop Doubting Yourself* than with a generic Word Document label. A title makes your book real. It gives you something to protect and nurture.

So it's time to create a title for your book. *My Fabulous Book* is pretty good as a document label, granted, but how about we shake things up? What's the name of your book? Sure, it's going to change by the time you're done, but let's get to know your baby on a first-name basis. That way, you won't be as tempted to throw it out with the bathwater when the going gets tough and chase after something that looks easier.

Need some ideas? Browse online bookstores for catchy titles or check out bestseller lists in your genre. Notice which titles catch your attention and which make you want to keep scrolling. If you want help creating a good title, you can download "Craft the Perfect Title for Your Prescriptive Nonfiction Book" in the bonus at www.summitpresspublishers.com/brick.

DO THIS

1. Create a title for your book. Even a working title gives your project more reality and keeps you committed to it.

2. Make a list of all the people you promise to offend with your writing; then take the list out into your backyard and burn it. You can't write the truth without ruffling some feathers.

3. Write a disclaimer for your book to protect the privacy of the people you'll write about.

4. Audit your information consumption. Are you researching or procrastinating? Pick one source of advice and stick with it.

5. Set boundaries around platform building. Choose one platform and commit to it rather than trying to be everywhere at once.

6. Remember that obstacles are part of the process, not evidence that you're doing something wrong. Every successful author has faced the same challenges you're facing right now.

14

GOOD GOD, I HAVE NO IDEA HOW TO WRITE

Learn the Craft Without Getting Trapped in Perpetual Student Mode

B y now, you've likely discovered something very important and very troubling. You've recognized that, to some degree, you have no idea what you're doing. And if you're writing stories from scratch? Whew, boy.

Maybe you're clueless about how to write dialogue that doesn't sound like robots having a committee meeting. Perhaps you're not entirely sure how to express your inner thoughts or use body language effectively. Or maybe you've got talking heads for thirty pages, and you can't get your characters away from that kitchen table. There they sit, yakking about the past, waving their coffee mugs in the air like some sort of animated book club.

Seems you haven't even gotten going yet, and you're up to your armpits in technical difficulties. These only serve to compound your emotional problems.

Congratulations. That's fantastic news! Because before you began this project, you had no idea what you didn't know. It all looked so damn easy. You've now graduated to an entirely different level. You've discovered that, to move forward, to finish your first shitty draft, you're going to have to learn something about the craft of writing.

If you've chosen to create something that requires serious skill development, you'll need to settle in for the long haul. You may not know it yet, but you're going to love this learning thing.

The $60,000 Truth About Learning to Write

All writers learn and do at the same time. Don't think for a minute that you need to put your project on hold until you've earned an MFA. To save you the $60,000 (inflation, my dear), I'd like to share what I learned at Harvard—the very principle each writing teacher emphasized at the start of the semester: "There is a school of thought that writing cannot be taught. Writing is learned by doing. The more you write, the better you get."

I'd like to modify that expensive statement: We learn best when we actually need to use what we've learned.

Mind you, enrolling in an MFA program is a terrific way to learn how to write, but there are other ways to develop your craft while working on your book without going into debt. Here are the options that actually work—and my take on what you should expect from each:

The Learning Menu (Choose Wisely)

Get a Writing Coach: Here's the deal: writing coaches vary dramatically in what they actually do, so don't just hire the first one with a nice website and good teeth. Some focus primarily on accountability, which is basically expensive cheerleading. Others act as thought partners in content development and strategy—that's where you get real value. Still, others specialize in specific genres or aspects of the publishing process.

If you want personalized, one-on-one attention with a strong focus on your work as you develop it, there's nothing better than hiring the right writing coach. But choose carefully. A good coach becomes your strategic partner. A mediocre one becomes an expensive friend who tells you your writing is "really coming along."

Take an Online Class: The online learning explosion has been both a blessing and a curse for writers. On the plus side, you can learn from authors like Malcolm Gladwell and Margaret Atwood through MasterClass without having to make small talk at faculty mixers. Udemy offers hundreds of writing courses at a fraction of university tuition costs. Coursera partners with top universities to deliver instruction that's actually useful.

The downside? You're on your own for motivation and accountability. If you're the type who buys gym memberships in January and cancels them by March, online classes might not be your best bet.

Join a Local Writing Class: College classes offer the benefit of in-person feedback and community, which means you can't hide behind your computer screen when it's time to share your work. Instructors present various aspects of craft and assign readings that will make you a better writer (whether you want to read them or not).

The real value is in the feedback sessions, where you'll discover that everyone struggles with the same issues you do. Teachers and classmates provide constructive criticism aimed at solving problems rather than destroying your soul. This is also a wonderful way to meet other writers who understand why you disappear for hours to wrestle with words.

Join a Writers' Group: Fair warning: the quality of these groups varies more wildly than airplane food. (I've got to say, Qatar Airways serves up awesome meals!) Some are fantastic communities of serious writers committed to improvement. Others feel more like group therapy sessions where everyone takes turns reading their feelings.

You'll find active communities on Facebook, Discord, Reddit, and specialized sites like Critique Circle and Scribophile. Some groups are private and selective; others will take anyone with a pulse and a laptop. Do your research before committing time to a group that spends more energy discussing their painful experience with rejection than improving their writing.

Learn from YouTube: This is where things get interesting. YouTube has become a goldmine of free writing instruction— if you know where to dig. Channels like Writing with Jenna

Moreci, Alexa Donne, and Brandon Sanderson's lectures offer university-level education at no cost.

But here's the thing: stick with creators who have actual publishing credentials, not just enthusiasm and a ring light. Look for instructors with expertise in your specific genre. Brandon Sanderson is impressive, but I doubt he'd have much to offer someone writing a business book about accounting practices.

Read Books on Craft: Every time I read about writing craft, I spot something I want to improve in my own work. My favorite craft book for beginners is Anne Lamott's *Bird by Bird*—she has a wonderful, funny way of breaking down writing components without making you feel like an idiot. For nonfiction writers, add *Several Short Sentences About Writing* by Verlyn Klinkenborg and *The Sense of Style* by Steven Pinker to your stack.

But heed my warning: don't become a craft book collector. You know the type—they have seventeen books about writing and zero finished manuscripts.

Read Strategically in Your Genre: Read as if you've never read before, especially books similar to what you're writing. Read to solve your own writing challenges. When you hit a section that works beautifully, stop and analyze why. When something feels off, figure out what the author did wrong so you can avoid the same mistake.

You get to be the judge and your own best teacher. Use other people's successes and failures as your free education.

Don't Overlook These Modern Resources

The learning landscape has changed dramatically since writers had to rely solely on university programs and dusty craft books. Some of these newer options can teach you more about actual reader preferences than traditional sources:

Leverage Reader Reviews for Education: Here's something they didn't teach in my expensive MFA program: Goodreads reviews provide wickedly honest reader reactions that can teach you more about writing than most craft books. When readers say, "I couldn't connect with the main character" or "This felt repetitive after chapter three," they're giving you free writing lessons.

Read reviews of books similar to yours and look for patterns in reader complaints. Do they consistently mention pacing issues, weak endings, or confusing structure? These are craft problems you can learn to avoid in your own work.

Learning Podcasts for Writers: Shows like *The Creative Penn*, *The Accidental Creative*, and *Grammar Girl* provide ongoing education you can consume while commuting. Just don't listen during your scheduled writing blocks—that's procrastination disguised as productivity. Bad.

The AI Truth Check: Let's address the elephant in the room: AI writing tools. Yes, ChatGPT can help with brainstorming and outlining. No, it cannot replace the thinking, experience, and insight that make your book valuable.

Use AI tools for what they excel at: generating ideas and identifying obvious errors. Don't use them to write your content. Readers can spot AI-generated text from outer space, and it sounds like every other generic book on the market. Plus, if AI is writing your book, what exactly are you bringing to the table?

Stop Learning Everything and Start Learning What Matters

Here's where most writers go horribly wrong: they try to learn everything about writing instead of focusing on what their specific project requires. It's like trying to become a master chef when all you need to do is make a decent grilled-cheese sandwich.

Fiction Writers: Master dialogue, character development, plot structure, and scene construction. Don't waste time on business writing techniques.

Memoir Writers: Focus on structuring life events into compelling narratives, balancing truth with storytelling needs, and handling sensitive material. Skip the vampire romance advice.

Business Writers: Learn to structure arguments clearly, write compelling case studies, and translate complex concepts into simple language. Most writers' groups will try to add more blood and fangs to your client success stories—ignore them.

Self-Help Writers: Master authentic transformation stories and credible case studies while avoiding new-age clichés that make readers roll their eyes.

The Learning Investment Balance

Regardless of your writer type, don't be cheap about your education, but also don't become a perpetual student. A $500 course that helps you finish your book is infinitely more valuable than free advice that keeps you stuck for another year.

Some writers collect courses and books about writing instead of actually writing. They become professional students who never graduate to professional authors. Set a learning budget and timeline, then get back to your keyboard. Make friends with that bad boy.

The best writing education comes from writing regularly and getting feedback from real readers in your target audience. All the craft instruction in the world won't help if you're not consistently putting words on the page.

DO THIS

1. Identify your biggest writing challenge and choose one specific resource to address it—this week, not next month.
2. Pick one learning method from the list above and commit to it for 30 days. Don't try to do everything at once.
3. Set boundaries around learning. Allocate specific time for education that doesn't come out of your writing time.
4. Join one writing community focused on your type of writing, but avoid groups that spend more time talking about writing than actually doing it.
5. Remember the goal: The best writing education comes from writing regularly and getting feedback from real readers, not from collecting courses like Pokémon cards.

15

UNTANGLING THE CHRISTMAS TREE LIGHTS

The Whole Revision Proccess

Let's say you've finally got yourself a complete first draft. Well, then, congratulations. Pat yourself on the back. You've just accomplished what 95 % of the folks who set out to write a book fail to do. This game is about pushing forward come hell or high water. It's about being okay with writing crap for a very long period. It's about ignoring your inner perfectionist and managing your doubts and impatience. It's about trusting that you'll iron out the wrinkles when the time comes.

You'll know when your shitty first draft is done when you've created all the content pieces you can think of, and you know (ish) what the book is about. For narrative works (memoirs, novels), this means you've written all the scenes and stories you can think of and have them arranged according to your outline. For prescriptive nonfiction (business, self-help, how-to books), this means you have your core framework in place, the main concepts you want to teach, the supporting research or data, the case studies or examples, and the stories that make it all relatable. Whether your bricks are primarily stories or primarily teaching content, you should, thanks to your outline, have them organized (ish).

You may be fidgeting in your seat right now because you recognize that your book isn't really a book yet. It has no flow to speak of, even though you've done everything you've been told to do. Nothing seems to fit quite right; there's no sense of cohesion.

It's hard not to worry. What if you've wasted all that time and energy for nothing? What if your project persists in looking like a steaming mound of ca-ca?

Hush, my pretty. A first draft is just the stuff you're going to use to create your book, nothing more, nothing less. At this point, it's not a novel, a memoir, an inspirational book, or whatever it is you decided to write. At this point, the very best it can be is a good slab of clay. And that's perfectly okay.

Welcome to the revision process.

The Christmas Tree Light Approach to Revision

Revision is a lot like untangling a solid ball of Christmas tree lights. When you first approach the mess, lying there on the floor just beneath the tree you're supposed to adorn, it seems unsalvageable—a gigantic waste of time and effort. Who the hell throws lights into a box like that? Collapsing, you scan the room looking for someone, anyone, whom you can blame.

But then you spot a single plug head sticking out. You grab hold of it, jiggle it, and lo and behold, one of the wires loosens up. Weaving the plug head in and out, suddenly the mass doesn't seem so impenetrable after all. An entire string separates from the whole. Armed with newfound patience, you tackle the bugger one string at a time until you've got them all lined up, ready to go. Problem solved.

That's exactly how you approach your manuscript revision. You don't try to fix everything at once—you'd go insane. You find one loose end and follow it through until you can separate out one complete "string" of your book. Then you tackle the next string, and the next, until you've got the whole thing untangled and working properly.

Here's your revision strategy: Start with the biggest, most obvious problems and work your way down to the smaller ones. Don't get distracted by a typo in Chapter 3 when the entire structure of your book needs work. Find the plug head, pull that string, untangle that mess, then move to the next string.

Your Revision Strings: Big to Small

String 1: The Big Picture Structure

Does your book have a clear beginning, middle, and end? Do your chapters flow logically from one to the next? Are you teaching concepts in the right order? Is your transformation story complete?

This is like checking whether your lights actually plug into the wall before you worry about individual bulbs.

String 2: Chapter-Level Problems

Now look at each chapter individually. Does every chapter serve a purpose? Do they each have a clear point? Are there chapters that could be combined or split up? Are there chapters that don't belong at all?

If you've been following the platform-building approach throughout this book, you've been testing your concepts with real readers as you wrote them. Now's the time to use that feedback. Which pieces of content got the strongest response? Which fell flat? Let your audience's reactions guide your revision decisions.

String 3: Content and Flow Within Chapters

Look at what's inside each chapter. For narrative works: Are your scenes vivid and purposeful? Do they advance the story or reveal character? For prescriptive nonfiction: Are your teaching points clear? Do your examples actually illustrate the concepts?

Every chapter needs to change the reader in some small way. If a chapter doesn't move your reader forward, it doesn't belong in your book.

String 4: The Language Level

Only after you've got your structure and content sorted should you worry about the actual words and sentences. This is where you read aloud, fix awkward phrasing, cut unnecessary words, and polish your voice.

Don't—and I cannot emphasize this enough—don't get caught up in perfecting sentences when your chapters are still in the wrong order. That's like polishing individual Christmas lights while they're still tangled in a ball.

Genre-Specific Revision Focus

Narrative Works (Memoir, Fiction)

Your main job is creating and maintaining narrative tension. Every scene needs conflict or change. If you have long passages where nothing happens in real time, you've got a problem.

Ask yourself: Does the story move logically from the first sentence to the last? Are your main events happening in scenes (showing) or in summary (telling)? Most successful narratives lean heavily toward showing.

The narrative arc is sacred—don't mess with it. You start with characters with problems, ramp up the complications until they come to a head, then resolve these complications or have your characters come to a new understanding of them. This shape has worked for thousands of years because it's how human brains process stories.

Prescriptive Nonfiction

Your main job is clarity and usefulness. For each chapter, you should be able to answer: What's the one main point? What story supports that point? What action do I want readers to take? How does this connect to the next chapter?

> If you can't answer those questions clearly, your readers won't be able to follow your logic.
>
> Use the feedback you've already collected from your platform-building efforts. Which concepts resonated? Which ones confused people? Which examples landed and which fell flat? Let your readers' reactions guide your revision decisions instead of guessing.

Deep Revision

Once you've untangled your major strings, it's time for the detailed work. This is where you let that inner perfectionist off the leash—but keep her focused on one task at a time.

Step 1. Read Your Manuscript Aloud

Read your piece aloud, sentence by sentence. Yes, this takes forever. You'll hear the awkward sentences, the tonal changes, and the places where you've got way too much explanation instead of story. You'll catch the clichés, overused expressions, and those adverbs that need to be doused in gasoline and burned.

Do this slowly, chunk by chunk. If you're responsible for putting young children to bed, why not kill two birds with one stone by using your manuscript as a bedtime story? Sure, you may overstimulate the little darlings with your riveting business transformation tale, but at least you'll know you're on the right track.

If you don't want to traumatize your children, record yourself reading your manuscript and play it back while you walk or do chores. You'll hear problems you miss when reading silently.

Step 2. The Theme Clarity Exercise

Read through your manuscript in one or two sittings and write a paragraph—no more than a third of a page—that summarizes what your book is about. This is the information you might put on the back cover.

This exercise is ridiculously hard, but push through it. With this summary in mind, go back through your manuscript chapter by chapter, cutting everything that doesn't support your central theme. Add scenes or examples that strengthen your main message.

This is where the magic happens—and where most writers quit because it's painful to cut material you worked hard to create. But this merciless editing is what transforms a pile of content into an actual book.

Step 3. The Bottom Drawer Test

When you think you're done with your masterpiece, grab it and stick it in a drawer. Leave it there for at least three months. This allows you the distance to see what you've really got.

Each time you revise, you'll be convinced of its brilliance because you'll have just blasted out some major problems. But until your work passes the drawer test, chances are you'll need at least one more major pass.

If you're the type who resists timeline delays, consider this the perfect opportunity to work on other projects, test additional content with your audience, or take a complete break from anything book-related.

The point is distance. You need fresh eyes, and that's impossible when you've been staring at your manuscript for months.

When Perfect Becomes the Enemy of Published

Here's the deal: You have more revision tools and feedback options than any previous generation of writers. You can get real-time input from your audience, access affordable professional help, and iterate based on actual reader reactions.

But all these options can also stymie you. You can spend months tweaking based on every piece of feedback you receive, or you can get so overwhelmed by revision possibilities that you never finish.

There's a good reason most worthwhile books take one to two years to write, including revision time. It takes time to get it right. Your book will come together if you stay at it.

But you also need to know when to stop. Perfect is the enemy of published. At some point, you need to call it done and get your book into the world where it can actually help people.

Remember: you're not writing the last book anyone will ever need on your topic. You're writing *your* book, with *your* perspective, for *your* readers. Done and published beats perfect and hidden every single time.

DO THIS

1. Identify your biggest structural problems first. Don't get distracted by typos when your chapters are in the wrong order.

2. Use the Christmas tree lights approach: Pull one string at a time. Fix structure, then content, then language.

3. Leverage the feedback you've already collected from your platform-building efforts. Let your readers' reactions guide your revision priorities.

4. Set a revision deadline. Give yourself a reasonable amount of time to revise, then stick to it.

5. Read your manuscript aloud once you've fixed the big problems. Your ears will catch what your eyes miss.

6. Put your finished manuscript in a drawer for at least three months before making your final decision about publication.

7. Remember that revision is where good books become great books. This is where you transform your pile of bricks into something readers will value and remember.

16

WHERE TO GO WHEN YOU'RE BLIND

When You Need Professional Help to See What You've Really Got

By now, you're probably saying, "Great, Ann, I've done all that revision stuff. And I've had it up to here with this tree because it's not coming down. Something's wrong, I think, but I don't quite know what."

I get it. It's easy to go blind to what you've got in hand. You've been looking at the same arrangement of words for so long that you don't know if you've created a bestseller or a more polished mound of crap. Without the necessary distance, it's hard to trust your own judgment. And it's not like your cat can read over your manuscript and give you useful feedback, even if it would like to.

When you're convinced you've done all you can do, when you're champing at the bit to get your book published, whom can you turn to? Who can save you from your own impatience and/or remarkable enthusiasm?

When I came out of writing school, my classmates and I often analyzed each other's work. One of us would mail her completed piece to the others, then wait a month or two for the package to be returned with a list of problems and recommendations spelled out in red ink. This editorial process took forever to complete. Still, we knew that if we did it for one, the favor would eventually be returned in kind. More importantly, we respected each other's opinions and skill sets, having witnessed them in writing workshops. We weren't just pals who'd met in some seedy bar.

While the audience feedback you've been collecting through your platform-building efforts can tell you where people got confused or bored, there comes a point where you need professional-level analysis. Your writing group buddies and newsletter subscribers can tell you what doesn't work, but they can't necessarily tell you how to fix structural problems or polish your prose to professional standards.

It's time to hand your manuscript over to a professional. Editing professionals—and we're going to talk about the different types in a moment—get paid to study your manuscript, point out problems, and offer corrective suggestions. Unlike your mother or best friends, these are people who'll have no trouble telling you the cold, hard truth. If you'd like to avoid the embarrassment and shame associated with publishing garbage, I can't recommend professional editing highly enough. Think of it as insurance for your professional reputation.

Types of Editing:
Know What You Need

There are primarily three (okay, maybe four) types of editing services in the publishing world, and understanding the difference can save you thousands of dollars and months of frustration.

Developmental Editing (The Big Picture)

What it is: Just like a good architect looks at the whole building before worrying about doorknob placement, developmental editing considers your entire manuscript—structure, flow, style, and tone—with an eye for overall soundness and readability.

Developmental editors are like manuscript therapists. They look for gaps that need filling, sections that need chopping, and themes that need supporting. They notice if that important character mentioned in chapter one disappears for two hundred pages, only to magically reappear when you remember you created him. They spot breaks in narrative perspective, dialogue that sounds stilted, and the desperate need for backstory that actually matters.

For prescriptive nonfiction, they can identify wonky frameworks, stories that lack clear points, and concepts that don't support your core message. They read for redundancies, inconsistencies, and believability. They analyze logic flow, missing steps, and conclusions that don't match your introductions.

What it costs: $2,000–$6,000, depending on the length and complexity of your manuscript. Yes, that's a lot of money. Yes, it's worth it if you're serious about your book.

When you need it: If you're writing anything with a narrative arc (memoir, novel) or a complex prescriptive book with multiple frameworks and moving parts. For simple how-to guides or straightforward motivational books, you can probably skip this level.

Red flag: Anyone offering developmental editing for under $1,000 is either inexperienced, working at unsustainable rates, or running a scam. Quality developmental editing takes weeks of focused work, not a weekend with a highlighter.

Book Doctoring (The Heavy Surgery)

What it is: This is when your manuscript needs more than feedback—it needs major reconstructive surgery. Book doctors don't just point out problems; they roll up their sleeves and rewrite sections of your manuscript, reorganize content, and essentially transform your rough material into a readable book. Think ghostwriting meets developmental editing.

When you need it: If you're a subject matter expert who struggles with writing, if English is your second language, if you've got brilliant content but can't make it flow, or if you've written something that reads more like detailed notes than an actual book.

What it costs: Roughly $10,000 to $20,000, depending on word count and how much rewriting is required. This isn't editing; it's essentially co-writing your book.

Critical requirement: You want someone who specializes in your genre. A book doctor who understands business books can't necessarily fix your memoir, and vice versa. The approaches are completely different, like asking a heart surgeon to fix your transmission.

Truth bomb: This is expensive because it's extensive work. If your budget can't handle this, you're better off spending more time improving your manuscript yourself before seeking professional help.

Copy Editing (The Line-by-Line Clean-Up)

What it is: Copy editors are the detail-obsessed people who go through your manuscript line by line, fixing your punctuation, grammar, and spelling. They make sure your syntax flows smoothly, your writing follows grammar conventions, your word choices are precise, and your punctuation is placed correctly.

They might also suggest some reorganization, recommend changes to chapter titles, and catch logic lapses or sequential inconsistencies. Think of them as your manuscript's personal trainer—they whip your writing into shape.

What it costs: $1,500 to $4,000 for a full manuscript, depending on how much work your writing needs. If English is your second language, budget toward the higher end.

When you need it: Everyone needs copy editing. Unless you're a professional editor yourself, your manuscript has errors you can't see. This is non-negotiable if you want to be taken seriously.

What you get: Your manuscript back with detailed notes and corrections, plus a list of diplomatic queries. For example: "Hey, you might want to consider taking the horns off the dog. Not sure dogs have horns." It's up to you to incorporate the suggested changes or not.

Proofreading (The Final Polish)

What it is: The final pass to catch typos, formatting issues, and any errors that slipped through copy editing. This is not a substitute for copy editing—it's the final step after everything else is complete.

What it costs: $500–$1,500 depending on length.

When you need it: After developmental editing and copy editing are complete and after you've made all your revisions.

Don't confuse this with copy editing: Proofreading assumes your content and structure are already solid. It's like the final car wash before you sell your vehicle, not the engine overhaul.

Where to Find Professional Editors (Without Getting Scammed)

Where once upon a time you had to know someone who knew someone who knew someone, the editing world has been completely transformed. You have more options than ever before, but you also have more ways to get scammed or waste your money.

The barrier to entry is so low that anyone can call themselves an editor, regardless of their actual skills. As a publisher, I've seen some pretty terrible "manuscript edits" that were basically expensive spell-checks.

Here's where to find the real professionals—and how to avoid the pretenders.

The Good Options

Reedsy.com: Probably the best platform for finding book professionals. Editors apply to be listed, so there's some quality control. You can see their experience, read reviews, and get quotes. Expect to pay market rates here—which is actually a good thing.

Professional Associations: Check the Editorial Freelancers Association (EFA) or similar organizations in your country. Members typically meet professional standards, which means they won't try to "edit" your memoir by adding more explosions.

Author Networks: Ask successful authors in your genre who they use. Most are happy to share recommendations, especially if you approach them respectfully and don't expect them to become your personal career counselor.

Industry Referrals: If you know anyone in the publishing world, ask for referrals. Personal recommendations from industry professionals are invaluable.

Proceed with Extreme Caution

Upwork.com: Massive freelance platform with editors from around the world. Quality varies like weather in springtime—

wildly unpredictable. You'll find experienced professionals charging appropriate rates, and you'll find people offering to "edit" your entire manuscript for $200. Guess which ones you should avoid.

Fiverr.com: Generally, avoid for serious editing work. The platform's race-to-the-bottom pricing attracts inexperienced editors and outright scammers. You get what you pay for, and $50 editing jobs deliver exactly $50 worth of value.

When to Run Away

The editing world is full of predators who prey on desperate authors. Here's how to protect yourself:

Promises to get you published: Editors edit. They don't guarantee publication. Anyone promising to get your book published is running a scam.

No samples or references: Any professional editor should be able to provide examples of their previous work and client references. If they can't or won't, walk away.

Unrealistic timelines: Quality editing takes time. Anyone promising to edit your manuscript in a week is either lying or running it through AI and calling it a day.

Prices too good to be true: If someone offers to developmentally edit your 300-page manuscript for $500, they're not doing developmental editing. They're taking your money and hoping you won't notice.

The Truth About AI and Professional Editing

Please, please, please. If you take away anything from this chapter, it's this: AI is not a replacement for professional developmental editing. AI can catch grammar errors and identify some structural issues, but it cannot judge whether your argument is compelling, your stories are engaging, or your voice is authentic.

Think of AI as an advanced spell-checker and research assistant. Use it to clean up obvious issues before you invest in professional editing, but don't mistake AI feedback for the nuanced judgment a human editor provides.

Red Flags to Avoid

Any service promising to "write your book with AI"—run away!

Claims that AI can replace professional editing—it cannot.

"AI-assisted publishing" that produces cookie-cutter content—your book will sound like everyone else's.

Any AI tool claiming to understand your industry better than you do—impossible.

The Economics of Editing: When It's Worth It (And When It's Not)

Let's talk dollars and sense. Professional editing isn't cheap, but it's an investment in your book's success and your professional reputation.

When to Invest in Full Professional Editing

If your book is central to your business strategy: You're using it to attract clients, establish expertise, or support speaking engagements.

If you're targeting traditional publishers: They expect professionally polished manuscripts. Submitting unedited work is professional suicide.

If you're building a platform: Your book represents your brand. Publishing something full of errors is like showing up to give a keynote in a tracksuit with coffee stains.

If you're writing narrative work: Novels and memoirs require developmental editing unless you're already an experienced writer.

When You Might Skip Professional Editing

Sometimes you don't need perfection—you need publication. Before you spend thousands on editing, honestly assess whether your book needs that level of investment.

Skip developmental editing if:

- You're writing simple, straightforward nonfiction (basic how-to guides, workbooks).
- You have extensive writing/editing experience.
- Your book is primarily a business card or lead magnet.
- You're testing market demand with a first book in a new area.

Skip professional editing entirely if:

- Your book serves a very specialized niche where domain expertise matters more than perfect prose.
- Your budget is truly limited (better to publish good enough than delay indefinitely).
- You're creating a simple client gift or internal company resource.

There's no shame in this approach if it serves your goals. Not every book needs to be a literary masterpiece. Some books just need to be good enough to do their job.

Working Effectively with Editors

Getting good value from professional editing requires being a good client. Here's how to make the process work:

Before You Hire

Be specific about what you want. Don't just say, "Edit my book," and expect the Red Sea to part. Specify whether you need developmental editing, copy editing, or both.

Ask for sample work. Professional editors should be able to show you examples of their previous work. Don't expect them to edit your pages for free—good editors are too busy for that game—but they should demonstrate their approach.

Discuss timelines realistically. Quality editing takes a minimum of two to four weeks. Plan accordingly and don't be that client who wants their 300-page manuscript back in three days.

Agree on scope upfront. What exactly will the editor deliver? Track changes? A style sheet? A summary letter? Get this in writing.

During the Process

Don't micromanage. Once you've hired an editor, let them work. Constant check-ins slow down the process and annoy your editor. And really, do you want to annoy the person holding a red pen to your manuscript?

Be open to feedback. You're paying for professional judgment. Don't argue with every suggestion—they're trying to help, not destroy your already shaky sense of self.

Ask about patterns. If your editor marks the same type of error repeatedly, ask how to avoid it in future writing.

After You Get Feedback

Don't implement every suggestion blindly. Good editors explain their reasoning. If you don't understand a suggestion, ask.

Focus on the big patterns. What systemic issues does your editor identify? These are learning opportunities that will improve all your future writing.

Budget for a second round. Major revisions often require another editing pass. This isn't failure—it's normal.

The Bottom Line

Professional editing can transform a good manuscript into a book you're confident putting your name on. It can save you from embarrassing errors, help you communicate more effectively, and give you the assurance that your work serves your readers well.

But editing is a tool, not a magic wand. It can't fix a book that has fundamental problems with concept, audience, or purpose. Make sure you've solved the big-picture issues before you invest in professional editing.

The goal isn't to create a flawless book—it's to create a book that does its job effectively. Whether that job is establishing your expertise, helping readers solve problems, or sharing insights that matter, professional editing helps ensure your message comes through clearly and professionally.

Now comes the fun part. You've identified your audience, gathered your material, structured your content, revised your manuscript, and potentially invested in professional editing. You've got a book—an actual, complete book that represents your expertise and serves your readers.

So what the hell do you do with it?

The publishing landscape offers more options than ever before, but it also presents more ways to waste time and money if you don't understand how the industry actually works. Let's talk about your real options for getting this thing published.

But first...

DO THIS

1. Decide what level of editing you actually need based on your book's purpose and your professional goals.

2. Research editors in your genre. Look at their experience, request samples, and verify references before you hand over your manuscript.

3. Budget realistically for editing services. Factor editing costs into your overall book budget from the beginning, not as an afterthought.

4. Start with AI tools to catch obvious errors before working with human editors. Clean up what you can first.

5. Be a good client. Communicate clearly, respect timelines, and be open to feedback. Your editor wants your book to succeed.

6. Remember that editing is an investment in your professional reputation and your book's success, not just an expense.

7. Don't let perfectionism paralyze you. Sometimes good enough really is good enough to get your book into the world where it can help people.

STEP 5

PUBLICATION
FOR DUMMIES

17

LAYOUT OF THE LAND

Navigate the Publishing Landscape Without Getting Scalped

We've covered choosing a genre, gathering clay, creating bricks, developing an outline, revising, and hiring professional help to polish your final draft. Now, my tenacious little beaver, we're going to explore the publishing landscape. This is where the tree meets the water—the outcome most of you have been working toward.

Listen up because I'm about to save you from some expensive mistakes.

The Publishing Revolution Nobody Talks About

The publishing landscape has undergone a dramatic transformation since the early 2000s. What was once a gatekeeping industry dominated by a handful of cigar-chomping New York publishers has evolved into a Wild West situation where anyone with a laptop can upload a book to Amazon with minimal effort.

Frankly, most of the advice you'll find online is either outdated or sheer bullshit written by people trying to sell you something—and I should know because I've been in this industry long enough to watch it turn inside out.

Expert Positioners and Practical Professionals—doctors, lawyers, consultants, coaches—are being told by business gurus that they need a book to build their platform, and they need it now. So they're rushing half-baked manuscripts to market without proper development or editing. What they end up with makes them look like rank amateurs in their own field. Their book becomes a liability rather than an asset.

But Beautiful Writers fall into the same trap for different reasons. While business professionals rush to market to capitalize on trends, Beautiful Writers often refuse to invest in professional help because they're banking on being "discovered" by traditional publishers. Just like Lana Turner at the soda fountain. They submit undercooked manuscripts to agents, get rejected, then wonder why their literary genius isn't being recognized.

Then there are the Influential Storytellers—those with powerful personal transformation stories who believe that raw authenticity automatically equals influence. They rush to share deeply personal content without considering whether their story serves readers beyond just being therapeutic for them to tell. The result? Memoir-style content that feels more like public journaling than strategic storytelling.

And then there are the Oprah Stage Dreamers—those who want massive reach and cultural impact. What they often miss: Oprah doesn't tout schlock. She champions books that are exceptionally well crafted, deeply researched, and professionally polished. When Oprah selects a memoir or transformational book, it's not just emotionally powerful—it's also structurally sound, expertly edited, and strategically positioned.

Amazon is positively drowning in books that read like they were written by caffeinated squirrels—approximately 4 million new books are published every year, most of which shouldn't exist. (I'll return to this theme throughout our publishing discussion because it's the single biggest factor affecting your book's success—and the biggest opportunity if you do things right.) The result? A credibility arms race where quality work gets lost in an ocean of garbage, and readers are becoming increasingly skeptical of all independently published work.

I witnessed this firsthand when a successful consultant hired me to help salvage his reputation after his DIY business book damaged his credibility with potential clients. We had to pull the book from circulation and start over—an expensive lesson in why shortcuts don't work when your professional reputation is on the line. (Yes, Rob, I'm talking about you.)

The Strategic Opportunity

Most people don't understand: the barrier to entry disappearing isn't necessarily bad news if you know how to navigate it strategically. The problem isn't that anyone can publish; it's that most people are making publishing decisions for emotional reasons rather than strategic ones.

The credibility crisis I mentioned? It's actually an opportunity for authors who do things right. When the market is flooded with junk, excellence stands out. When everyone else is cutting corners, investing in professional development and editing becomes a competitive advantage. When other authors are making emotional decisions, methodical thinking sets you apart.

Your Three Paths Forward

You have three fundamental publishing options, each serving different goals:

Traditional Publishing: offers maximum credibility and distribution but requires steep entrance requirements and lengthy timelines.

Partnership/Hybrid Publishing: provides professional quality with author control for upfront investment.

Self-Publishing: gives maximum control and profit potential but requires managing everything yourself.

Notice I didn't mention which one is "best." That's because the best option depends entirely on your goals, timeline, budget, and platform.

Beautiful Writers often assume traditional publishing is the only legitimate path because it offers literary credibility. Expert Positioners and Practical Professionals typically find hybrid publishing ideal because it gives them control over timeline and messaging while ensuring professional quality. Oprah Stage Dreamers need to understand that massive cultural impact requires exceptional content combined with strategic platform building—and often significant financial investment in professional support.

The Upshot

Your book is not your baby. It's a business tool. Treat it like one. Invest appropriately, set clear expectations, and for the love of all that's holy, hire an editor before you inflict your first draft on the world.

What I've learned after helping hundreds of authors navigate this landscape—there are no shortcuts to credibility, and there's no substitute for doing the work right the first time. I'm sorry, I wish there were.

The following three chapters will give you the unvarnished truth about each publishing path—what they actually cost, how long they really take, and which one serves your specific goals. No marketing puffery, no fairy tales, just the facts you need to make a smart business decision.

DO THIS

1. Review your Why. Has it changed since you started this journey? Choose a publishing path that aligns with your actual objectives.

2. Accept that publishing is a business decision, not a creative one. Your ego doesn't get a vote.

3. Identify your real goal before choosing a publishing path. Be specific about what success looks like.

4. Prepare to invest appropriately in whichever path you choose. Excellence costs money, and shortcuts cost credibility.

18

THE BIG LEAGUE

When Traditional Publishing Still Makes Sense (And When It Doesn't)

Once upon a time—before the success of wholesalers like Amazon and the advent of eBooks—traditional publishing houses were the only game in town. If you wanted your book in print, you had to traverse an alligator-infested moat to bang on their castle door. Now, of course, that's no longer the case. You don't need to run their gauntlet to be chosen as one of the lucky few.

Yet, traditional publishing remains the gold standard for author credibility and widespread distribution. But before you start fantasizing about book tours and literary awards, you need to understand what you're actually signing up for. I'm not going to walk you through every detail of the submission process—that's a book in itself—but I'll give you enough information to make an educated choice about whether this path aligns with your goals and timeline.

Now, the publishing industry's response to the flood of low-quality self-published content has been to raise the drawbridge even higher. Faced with millions of amateur books vying for attention, traditional publishers have doubled down—they're more selective than ever, taking zero risks and acting like exclusive nightclub bouncers who only let in people who are already famous. Britney Spears? C'mon in. Ralph Smith? Nice try, buddy.

But some authors still want to play in the big leagues. I get it. There's something undeniably sexy about having Penguin Random House or Simon & Schuster on your book spine. For certain authors—particularly those seeking maximum credibility or retail distribution—traditional publishing may still be worth the hassle.

Notice I said, "may be." Because let me tell you what traditional publishing actually looks like these days, and it's not the fantasy most people harbor.

The New Publishing Equation

Traditional publishing houses have become venture capitalists in book form. They're not looking for good writers; they're looking for safe bets. The Big Five—Penguin Random House, HarperCollins, Macmillan, Simon & Schuster, and Hachette—are essentially risk-averse corporations that have figured out it's easier to buy success than to create it.

This wasn't always the case. These conglomerates used to have huge sales forces, public relations teams, and design staffs working around the clock promoting books and authors. But then the industry crashed, folks got laid off, and resources were cut to the bare bone. Authors could no longer leave book promotion to publishers; they were compelled to spend significant time and energy marketing their books—particularly on social media—in order to remain on those coveted shelves.

What does this mean for you today? They want authors who can guarantee book sales through existing platforms and proven track records. They're not interested in developing new talent; they want to acquire existing success—kind of like dating someone who's already married.

Literary agent Lucinda Halpern, in her book *Get Signed*, offers a helpful framework for understanding what agents and acquisition editors at these big houses actually look for. According to Halpern, you need at least two of three key qualities:

1. **A Big Idea** (a compelling, marketable concept),
2. **A Platform** (an engaged audience or established credibility),
3. **Excellent Writing** (craft that serves your content effectively).

This explains why some beautifully written books get rejected while others with strong platforms but weaker prose get deals. The powers that be are all looking for the combination that gives a book the best chance of commercial success.

For Beautiful Writers without platforms, this framework reveals a harsh truth: you better have both a big idea and excellent writing, and you better be willing to invest years perfecting both. One of my graduate school instructors, Paul Harding, exemplifies what this looks like in practice. He spent seven grueling years working on a novel, continually throwing his drafts in the dumpster and starting again from scratch because his goal was to create something lasting and beautiful. He refused to let market pressure influence his work. (If you're in academia, you know the drive to publish or perish, which doesn't lend itself to patience.) In 2010, years after I'd graduated, Paul Harding won a Pulitzer Prize in fiction for his first novel, *Tinkers*.

This proves that if you want to break through traditional publishing as a complete unknown, exceptional craft combined with a compelling concept can still work—but you're looking at years of development, not months. Harding's success also shows the kind of dedication required when you're competing purely on the strength of your writing rather than your platform.

The Agent Gauntlet

If you do have the platform to justify traditional publishing interest, you'll need an agent. Period. The Big Five publishers no longer accept unsolicited manuscripts from authors—you must have representation. (Some smaller traditional publishers still accept direct submissions, but they're increasingly rare and typically have much smaller distribution reach.)

This means that agents are the gatekeepers to the gatekeepers.

Finding an agent, you should know, is like online dating but with more rejection and less chance of a happy ending. You'll craft query letters—essentially cover letters for your book—and send them to agents who specialize in your genre. Most will ignore you. Some will send form rejections. A few might ask for sample chapters.

Here's where the rest of the process diverges based on what you're writing:

For nonfiction authors: If an agent shows interest, they'll then want a book proposal—essentially a business plan for your book that's a beast to create. We're talking 60-80 pages of meticulously crafted content that includes market analysis, competitive analysis, detailed marketing plans, chapter-by-chapter outlines, sample chapters, your complete bio and platform details, and sales projections.

For novelists: Agents will want to see your completed manuscript, a compelling synopsis (typically 1-2 pages that summarizes your entire plot including the ending), and your query letter. You won't need a full book proposal, but you'll need to have finished the entire novel. No exceptions.

For memoirists: This gets tricky. Memoir falls into a gray area between fiction and nonfiction. Some agents treat memoir like fiction and will want a completed manuscript plus synopsis. Others treat it like nonfiction and will want a book proposal with sample chapters and an outline of remaining chapters. The key difference? Memoir proposals often require more of the book to be written than other nonfiction—typically 50-75% completed rather than just sample chapters.

Think writing your book was hard? Try writing a book proposal. It requires completely different skills—part marketing document, part academic thesis, part sales pitch. Most authors require professional assistance to craft compelling proposals, which typically costs $3,000-$18,000 and takes two to four months to create properly.

And here's the kicker: even with a brilliant proposal, most agents will still pass. You're essentially paying thousands of dollars for the privilege of maybe getting rejected more expensively.

The Financial Reality

Now, let's talk money because this is where most authors' dreams go to die a slow and painful death.

Yes, you might get an advance. For first-time authors without celebrity status, we're talking $5,000-$15,000 if you're lucky. Most never see another penny beyond that advance because their books don't sell enough copies to "earn out."

Let's do some quick math. If your book sells for $20 and you get a 10% royalty, you're making $2 per book. To earn out a $10,000 advance, you need to sell 5,000 copies. The problem? The average traditionally published book sells fewer than 1,000 copies total.

Remember, the publisher controls everything—cover design, title, marketing budget, distribution, pricing, even whether your book stays in print. You become a minority stakeholder in your own intellectual property.

I've seen larger advances—the biggest was $250,000, which sounds life-changing until you hear the rest of the story. This went to an author with a massive platform and proven sales in her field. Every penny of that advance went right back into marketing the book so she could meet the sales commitments she'd made to the publishing house. The publisher essentially lent her money to market her own book. She also had to hire an outside editor because the internal editor was too busy to work with her on content development.

So much for the daydream of having your own dedicated editor pouring you tea and holding your hand through the process.

Nutshell? Choose traditional publishing for credibility and distribution, not for money.

Why Anyone Still Chooses This Path

So why would anyone choose traditional publishing? Three compelling reasons:

1. **Credibility:** There's still a perception that traditionally published authors are more "legitimate." This matters in academic circles, for speaking bureaus, and when positioning yourself as a thought leader.
2. **Distribution:** Traditional publishers have relationships with bookstores, libraries, and institutional buyers that are difficult to replicate independently. They maintain deep connections and purchasing systems that store

and library buyers trust, which translates to highly visible shelf space for your book. Despite the growth of online sales, if you want your book in airport bookstores and Barnes & Noble, traditional publishing is still your best bet.

3. **Validation:** Sometimes, you need the external validation of a major publisher to convince others (including yourself) that your ideas have merit. There's nothing wrong with wanting that stamp of approval.

For Oprah Stage Dreamers seeking massive cultural impact, traditional publishing becomes almost mandatory. Oprah's Book Club historically selects from traditionally published titles—if you're dreaming of that level of mainstream recognition and cultural influence, traditional publishing may be your only viable path despite all its challenges.

The Strategic Decision

Traditional publishing is not about your worth as a writer or the quality of your ideas. It's about market conditions, timing, and whether your existing platform can guarantee sales. Don't take rejection personally, even if you'd like to, and don't assume acceptance means you're a better writer than someone who chose a different path.

The question isn't whether you're "good enough" for traditional publishing. The question is whether traditional publishing serves your goals better than the alternatives, and whether you have the right combination of Halpern's three elements: Big Idea, Platform, and Writing quality.

Traditional publishing might be right for you if you already have a substantial platform, credibility and prestige matter more than profit or control, you want maximum retail distribution, you're willing to wait 18 to 24 months to see your book in print, you don't mind giving up creative and business control, your book fits neatly into a currently popular category, and you have the time and money to invest in the query/proposal process.

If you're writing a business book tied to current market conditions or need your book for speaking engagements that are already booked, traditional publishing timelines will murder your momentum. By the time your traditionally published book arrives, your industry will have moved on to the next trend. You'll be selling skinny jeans in an era of wide-leg everything.

Even traditional publishers know this is a problem. That's why many are now launching their own hybrid imprints—they're quietly admitting that the old way of doing business doesn't work for most authors or most books. That should tell you everything you need to know about the current state of traditional publishing.

DO THIS

1. Honestly assess your platform. Do you have the kind of engaged audience that actually buys your products or services?

2. If yes, research agents who represent books in your category and budget for professional query letter and book proposal development.

3. If no, stop fantasizing about traditional publishing and focus on options that actually serve your goals.

4. Remember: Rejection from traditional publishers says nothing about your worth as a writer or the value of your ideas.

19

THE SWEET SPOT

Why Hybrid Publishing Works When You Need Control and Quality

For most professionals writing nonfiction books, hybrid publishing is like ordering à la carte at a restaurant instead of accepting whatever the chef decides to serve you or trying to cook a five-course meal yourself when you can barely boil an egg. You get exactly what you want, prepared by professionals, without surrendering control over the final product.

Let me clear up some terminology confusion first. "Hybrid publishing" has become the standard term for what used to be called "partnership publishing." Some companies also call it "author-assisted publishing," though that term sometimes includes lower-quality services we'll help you avoid. Don't let anyone tell you these are different things—they're not. Same model: you invest in your book's production, maintain ownership and control, and work with publishing professionals who have skin in the game.

If you've been following along since Chapter 17, you know each publishing path serves different goals. For Expert Positioners and Practical Professionals who need credible, professional-quality books that enhance their business objectives, hybrid publishing hits the sweet spot between traditional publishing's loss of control and self-publishing's overwhelming complexity.

Why Hybrid Makes Sense

Think of hybrid publishing as the Goldilocks option—not too corporate, not too chaotic, but just right for professionals who understand their book is a business tool.

Like traditional publishing, you get professional editing, design, and distribution. Like self-publishing, you maintain control and keep the lion's share of profits. But here's what makes hybrid unique: you get the selectivity and professional standards of traditional publishing combined with the control and higher royalties of self-publishing.

Quality hybrid publishers have submission processes, standards, and reputations to protect. When we consider a manuscript at Summit Press Publishers, for example, we're evaluating three things: the author's platform, the book's market potential, and whether the content meets professional standards. If a manuscript doesn't meet the standards, it gets turned away. This selectivity benefits you because your book gets associated with other quality titles, not the vanity press garbage flooding Amazon.

What Your Investment Actually Buys

Let's talk money because this isn't charity—it's a business arrangement that should benefit both parties.

When you work with a quality hybrid publisher, you're hiring a general contractor who manages a team of publishing professionals. Instead of you trying to find, vet, and coordinate editors, designers, formatters, and distributors, the publisher handles all that using proven professionals they work with regularly.

You're looking at $12,000-$25,000, which includes:

- Professional development and copy editing
- Interior and cover design
- Multiple format creation (print, e-book, sometimes audiobook)
- ISBN assignment and distribution setup
- Initial marketing optimization
- Ongoing royalty reporting and payment

Here's what you don't get, and this is crucial: they don't do your marketing for you. You're still responsible for building your platform, driving sales, and promoting your book. What they do is create a professional product and make it available through major distribution channels.

Many hybrid publishers offer additional marketing services, but understand that everyone's marketing needs are different. Your promotion strategy has to reflect your unique situation and objectives, not some cookie-cutter approach.

The Timeline Advantage

Remember how traditional publishing takes 18 to 24 months? Hybrid publishing typically takes 3 to 4 months from final manuscript to published book. This matters if you're launching a business, building a speaking career, or responding to current market conditions.

I've seen authors use their books to land speaking engagements that pay more than their entire publishing investment. Try doing that with traditional publishing's timeline.

Yes, you're investing significant money upfront. But unlike traditional publishing, you're not giving away your rights or future profits.

Here's how the math actually works. One author invested $15,000, then ordered 500 copies at cost to sell at speaking engagements for $25 each. She made $12,500 selling those books, covering most of her investment while earning quarterly royalty checks from other channels. Within six months, she'd recouped her investment and built a steady revenue stream.

Compare that to traditional publishing, where you might get a $10,000 advance (if you're lucky) and never see another penny.

Avoiding the Predators

The hybrid space is positively crawling with wolves in sheep's clothing—vanity presses that rebranded themselves as "hybrid publishers." They're counting on your ignorance to separate you from your money.

Red flags to watch for:

- Companies accepting every manuscript without review
- Unrealistic promises about sales without explaining required investment and strategy
- Exclusive long-term contracts
- Publishers who won't provide references from other authors
- Existing catalogs that look unprofessional

And whatever you do, don't fall for "AI-assisted" publishing services promising to write or heavily edit your book using artificial intelligence. These services produce generic, soulless content that reads like it was churned out by a perpetually bored committee housed in a cinderblock building. Your book's value comes from your scars, failures, and breakthrough moments. AI cannot replicate that.

Legitimate hybrid publishers like Greenleaf Book Group, Page Two, She Writes Press, and Summit Press Publishers stake their reputations on quality work. We have curated catalogs, selective acceptance processes, and authors who are happy to discuss their experiences.

When Hybrid Works (and When It Doesn't)

Hybrid publishing works well if you:

- Want professional quality without surrendering control
- Need your book within 3 to 4 months rather than years
- Have a business or practice the book will support

- Want to keep the majority of your profits
- Don't want to manage multiple freelancers yourself
- Value being associated with other quality titles

It's wrong for you if you:

- Expect the publisher to market your book
- Don't have a budget for upfront investment
- Want maximum prestige from traditional publishing
- Aren't willing to be actively involved in the process

Beautiful Writers seeking literary recognition might find traditional publishing more aligned with their goals. Similarly, Oprah Stage Dreamers should understand that major platforms like Oprah's Book Club historically select from traditionally published titles—so if mainstream recognition is your goal, traditional publishing may be necessary despite its challenges.

The Long-Term Relationship

Most authors don't consider what happens after publication. Traditional publishers move on to their next season and forget about your book. Self-published authors are entirely on their own.

Quality hybrid publishers maintain ongoing relationships with their authors. We handle royalty reporting, assist with reprints, and provide guidance about using your book strategically in your business.

Your book becomes a cornerstone of your professional platform, not just a one-time project gathering dust. I've seen authors leverage their books to secure higher speaking fees, attract better clients, land media interviews, establish industry thought leadership, and create additional revenue streams.

The Strategic Investment

Hybrid publishing isn't the cheapest option, but it's often the smartest for professionals who understand that quality requires investment.

You're not paying for the privilege of being published—you're investing in a business asset that should pay dividends for years. Choose wisely, work with reputable companies, and remember that no publisher can turn weak content into a strong book. But the right hybrid publisher can turn strong content into a professional product that serves your goals and enhances your reputation.

Don't let anyone convince you that cheaper is better when it comes to your professional credibility. Your book will either enhance or damage your reputation. There's no middle ground.

DO THIS

1. Research hybrid publishers whose catalogs align with your genre and goals—look at their actual books, not just their websites.

2. Ask for references from other authors and actually contact them. Ask about the experience, not just the outcome.

3. Get detailed proposals from 2 to 3 companies before making a decision. Compare what's included and what costs extra.

4. Budget for the full investment, including any optional marketing services you might want.

5. Remember: you're investing in a business asset that should generate returns, not buying a service to make you feel good about yourself.

20

GOING IT ALONE

When Self-Publishing Makes Sense (And How to Do It Right)

Self-publishing is both the most accessible and the most dangerous path in modern book publishing. Like I've said a million times: Anyone with a laptop can upload a document to Amazon and call themselves a published author—which is exactly the problem. The question is whether you want to join the ranks of professionals using self-publishing strategically or become another cautionary tale about cutting corners. *Poor Jack. Remember when we thought he was up and coming?*

Let me be clear about something online gurus conveniently forget to mention: self-publishing is not the easy button. Yes, anyone can upload their grocery list to Amazon and slap a $2.99 price tag on it. But creating a book that actually serves your professional goals? That requires the same level of investment and strategic thinking we've been discussing throughout this book.

And. There are advantages to self-publishing. You have complete control over every decision—cover design, pricing, marketing, distribution, even whether your book stays in print. The disadvantage? You're responsible for every decision, and most authors aren't prepared for what that actually means. It's like being handed the keys to a fighter jet when you've never flown anything more complicated than a paper airplane.

Your Two Roads
(Because Life Loves Choices)

Most wannabe authors stumble into self-publishing without understanding that there are two completely different approaches, and confusing them can cost you thousands of dollars and months of frustration. It's like showing up to a black-tie event in cargo shorts—technically, you're dressed, but you're missing something crucial.

Road One: True DIY Self-Publishing (The Control Freak's Paradise)

This means you manage every aspect yourself—you're the author, publisher, project manager, and quality control department all rolled into one. Think general contractor meets perfectionist meets someone who clearly has too much time on their hands.

You hire individual freelancers for editing, cover design, interior formatting, and any other services you need. You coordinate their work, manage timelines, and make all creative and business decisions. You also get to keep all your rights and the lion's share of profits from sales, which is nice if your book actually sells.

Amazon KDP (Kindle Direct Publishing) is where most self-published books live and die. You upload your files, set your price, and Amazon handles printing and shipping when customers place orders. For broader distribution, you can use IngramSpark, which gets your book into bookstores and libraries that Amazon doesn't reach—assuming anyone actually wants to stock it.

Quality DIY self-publishing typically costs $3,000-$5,000 if you hire professional help. You could spend less, but remember—your book represents you professionally. Nobody's going to cut you slack because you went cheap on editing.

DIY makes sense if you actually enjoy project management (weird, but some people do), want maximum control over every decision, have time to research and vet freelancers, don't mind coordinating multiple moving parts, and want to keep the highest percentage of profits.

It's a terrible choice if you hate managing details, don't have time to learn publishing logistics, get overwhelmed coordinating multiple people, or want someone else to handle the complexity while you focus on your actual business.

Road Two: Self-Publishing Services (Hiring Someone Who Knows What They're Doing)

Before we dive in, let's clear up some confusion: don't mistake self-publishing services for hybrid publishing. With self-publishing services, you're buying coordination help but keeping 100% of your rights and royalties. With hybrid publishing, you're entering a partnership where the publisher takes ongoing royalties in exchange for being selective and having skin in the game. Think of self-publishing services as hiring a wedding planner—they coordinate everything you've chosen from their menu, but it's still your potentially ill-advised choice of spouse, your wedding, and your money.

These companies offer various package deals that handle most of the publishing process for you. You pay a fee, they coordinate some level of editing and design, and you get a finished book. Sounds simple, right? The devil, as always, is in the details—and sometimes the devil is wearing a three-piece suit and a convincing smile.

The best self-publishing services are like hiring a general contractor who actually shows up and does quality work. Companies like Reedsy, BookBaby, and Girl Friday Productions have established solid reputations by maintaining quality standards and working with experienced freelancers who won't make your book look like it was designed by someone's nephew "who's good with computers."

The worst are predatory vanity presses disguised as publishing services. They make unrealistic sales promises, try to lock you into exclusive agreements, and produce books that look like...yah, that nephew I mentioned.

Here's how to tell them apart: legitimate services are transparent about their process, provide samples of their work that don't make you cringe, don't make sales promises that sound like lottery ticket commercials, allow you to retain all rights, and don't require exclusive long-term contracts that would make a cell phone company jealous.

Quality services typically charge $4,000-$12,000, depending on what's included. The question is whether you're getting value for that investment or just paying someone to coordinate the same freelancers you could hire yourself for half the price.

The Marketing Wake-Up Call (This Is Where Dreams Go to Die)

Here's where most self-published authors face a rude awakening: you're responsible for every single sale. Amazon isn't going to promote your book unless you're already selling thousands of copies (catch-22, anyone?). Barnes & Noble isn't featuring unknown authors unless you're somebody's cousin or you've got serious marketing muscle behind you.

If you don't drive traffic to your book, it disappears into the millions of other titles competing for attention faster than your motivation on a rainy Monday morning.

This is why I've been stressing throughout this book the importance of building your platform while you write. Self-published authors who ignored that advice suddenly realize they have no audience waiting for their book. They're starting their marketing from scratch, trying to find readers who don't know they exist and frankly don't care.

Authors with established platforms have readers actively searching for their work. Those without platforms are hoping strangers stumble across them by accident—which is about as effective as waiting for Publishers Clearing House to show up at your door.

Mind you, some self-published authors have cracked the code and generate substantial income. They understand Amazon's algorithms, keyword strategies, and promotional tactics that most authors never learn. But their success comes from treating book marketing like a full-time job, because that's essentially what it is.

When Self-Publishing Actually Works

Nutshell. Self-publishing can be brilliant if you've built a substantial platform, enjoy marketing and promotion (or at least don't break out in hives at the thought of it), want complete control over pricing and distribution, need your book available quickly, have realistic expectations about sales, and are willing to treat book marketing as an ongoing commitment rather than a one-time announcement.

It's a disaster if you expect the book to market itself, lack time or interest in promotion, want someone else to handle business aspects, need external validation for your work, or believe that publishing equals automatic sales and passive income.

For Beautiful Writers or Influential Storytellers, self-publishing offers complete creative control but requires exceptional marketing skills to build readership. For Expert Positioners and Practical Professionals, it works when you have existing clients and speaking opportunities that create built-in demand. Your book becomes an expensive business card that generates revenue through related services rather than direct sales. Oprah Stage Dreamers? We've already established where you need to be. And it ain't here.

Beyond Book Sales (Where the Real Money Lives)

Smart self-published authors don't just sell books—they build business ecosystems. Your book becomes the foundation for online courses, speaking engagements, consulting opportunities, and other revenue streams that make book royalties look like pocket change.

I've seen self-published authors use their books to command five-figure speaking fees, attract premium consulting clients, and build online communities around their expertise. But they didn't start marketing after publication—they built their platforms while writing and treated their book as one component of a larger business strategy, not the entire strategy.

The Investment 411

Self-publishing isn't cheaper than other publishing paths when done professionally—it's just structured differently. Instead of paying a hybrid publisher upfront, you're investing in individual services and taking on the coordination responsibility yourself. It's like choosing to renovate your own house instead of hiring a contractor—you might save money, but you're definitely not saving time or sanity.

The question isn't whether to invest money—professional quality requires professional investment regardless of your publishing path. The question is whether you want to manage that investment yourself or pay someone else to coordinate it while you focus on things that actually generate income.

Making the Call

Choose DIY self-publishing if you want maximum control and are prepared to manage complexity that would make air traffic controllers nervous. Choose self-publishing services if you want coordination help while retaining ownership. Avoid vanity presses like you'd avoid a timeshare presentation—they'll promise you the world and deliver a desperate desire to escape.

Most importantly, remember that publishing your book is just the beginning. Success in self-publishing comes from what you do after publication, not before. The real work starts when you have to convince people to actually read the damn thing.

DO THIS

1. Decide your approach: DIY coordination or hiring a service—but research the difference between legitimate services and vanity presses that would publish your grocery list for the right price.

2. If hiring a service, research their reputation like you're hiring someone to watch your kids. Demand work samples, ask for author references you can actually contact, and scrutinize the fine print.

3. Budget appropriately: Professional quality requires professional investment, regardless of your publishing path. Your book represents you—invest accordingly.

4. Develop your marketing plan now, not after publication when panic sets in. Your platform-building work becomes crucial for self-publishing success.

5. Remember: You're building a business asset that needs to generate returns on your investment, not just publishing a book to make your mother proud.

CONCLUSION

Alright, my tenacious little beavers, let's talk about what you've accomplished by making it this far. As I said at the beginning, most people who talk about writing a book never make it past the cocktail party conversation stage. Those people? They're still bleaching grout and grooming unicorns while you've been building something real.

You've moved beyond wishful thinking into strategic action—and more importantly, you understand that your book and your platform aren't separate projects competing for your attention. They're one integrated system, like coffee and morning productivity, or binge-watching and avoiding actual work.

What You Actually Know Now (No Corporate Buzzwords, I Promise)

This isn't just another writing book that sends you off to suffer in isolation, living on instant ramen and delusions of literary grandeur. You've learned to think strategically about content creation while building relationships with your future readers.

First, you figured out which of the five major writer types you are—Beautiful Writers seeking artistic recognition, Expert Positioners building expertise-based businesses, Practical Professionals enhancing their careers, Influential Storytellers sharing transformative life experiences, or Oprah Stage Dreamers aiming for massive cultural impact. Understanding your type isn't just nice-to-know information; it drives every strategic decision you make, from genre choice to publishing path to platform-building approach.

You discovered you're probably sitting on a content goldmine without even knowing it. Through our scavenger hunt approach, you learned to mine your existing emails, presentations, social media posts, client work, and conversations for book material. No more starting from ground zero—you already have more content than you think.

You understand the brick system: instead of staring at a blank page wondering how the hell you're supposed to write an entire book, you write one manageable piece at a time. One story. One framework. One case study. Each brick is completable, achievable, and moves you forward without the paralysis that comes from contemplating the enormity of "writing a book."

And here's what many writing guides miss: you understand that story is the glue that holds books together, regardless of genre. Whether you're writing business nonfiction, memoir, or prescriptive content, the ability to craft compelling narratives—with real characters facing real conflicts in specific settings—transforms dry information into memorable, useful content that actually changes readers.

You've learned that different genres require different architectural blueprints. Memoir structure differs fundamentally from prescriptive nonfiction, which differs from narrative nonfiction. You have genre-specific outlining strategies and templates that ensure your bricks build something cohesive rather than just a pile of good content that makes little if any sense when assembled.

But here's the really powerful part: you've learned to create sophisticated outlines that show you exactly where each content brick belongs. Your approach to structure means you're building with purpose, not just hoping everything will somehow fit together in the end. Even your working title keeps the project feeling real and achievable rather than some vague, overwhelming concept.

And here's the modern advantage that previous generations of writers didn't have: you understand that book writing isn't about disappearing for two years hoping your ideas work. You test and refine your content with real audiences as you create it, discovering what resonates before investing months in a full manuscript. Yay, you!

What Happens Next (And Why You're Ready for It)

You have significant work ahead, but you're approaching it strategically instead of wandering around like a confused tourist in a Moroccan bazaar.

You understand revision as a well-planned process, not just cleanup duty. You know the difference between revising simple structural books versus complex prescriptive nonfiction, and you have genre-specific approaches for making your content stronger. You'll revise extensively because good books become great books in revision—not because you're a perfectionist with control issues. Even if that's true.

Most importantly, you've discovered that the publishing industry's traditional advice is backwards. Platform building doesn't happen after publication—it happens during content creation. This isn't an add-on to the writing process. It *is* the writing process.

You'll invest in professional developmental editing because your book represents your professional reputation. There's no room for amateur work when your credibility is at stake, and sorry, but your English teacher friend who offers to "take a look" doesn't count as professional editing.

Then you'll make a publishing decision based on your goals, timeline, and resources—not because one path sounds cooler at dinner parties. You know the real costs, timelines, and trade-offs. You'll choose based on what serves your objectives, not ego.

The Part Where I Don't Blow Sunshine

Let me cut through the industry nonsense about what's still ahead. The publishing landscape is more challenging than ever. You're competing not just with other books, but with every piece of content your audience consumes—podcasts, social media, Netflix, that fascinating article about why cats knock things off tables. (I've always chalked that up to aggression.)

Your book needs to deliver genuine value, not just rehash ideas that already exist everywhere online. This means you can't coast on good intentions or artistic temperament. Your content must solve real problems for real people. Your stories must illuminate universal truths, not just provide personal therapy sessions for your childhood issues.

But here's the thing: you're prepared for this because you recognize that connecting with readers is part of the creative process, not an annoying afterthought that somehow taints your artistic purity.

Beyond Just Publishing a Book (The Real Payoff)

Your book is just the beginning of your strategic content system, not the end goal. The Expert Positioners I work with use their books to command higher consulting fees, attract premium clients, and land keynote speaking engagements. The Beautiful Writers discover that understanding their audience enhances rather than compromises their artistic vision. The Practical Professionals find that their industry-focused books open career doors that decades of traditional networking couldn't access. The Influential Storytellers leverage their books to build movements and create lasting social impact. The Oprah Stage Dreamers understand that books open doors, but ongoing valuable content keeps those doors open.

Your book becomes your ambassador to the world, your credibility-building tool, and your door-opener to opportunities you can't yet imagine. But only if people actually read it. Only if you finish it with professional quality standards. Only if you treat it as the strategic decision it is.

Time to Take That First Bite

Quit stalling and start creating content. You have everything you need to begin building your content ecosystem. Your book won't write itself while you attend more webinars about writing books. Your platform won't build itself while you research platform-building methods for the next six months. Your professional credibility won't establish itself while you analyze what successful authors did ten years ago in a completely different market.

You can join the millions who talk about writing books but never finish them, or you can join the small percentage who understand that building books brick by brick—with clear thinking, professional quality standards, and integrated platform development—creates books that get read, remembered, and produce results.

You have your content brick approach. You understand your outlining system. You know the real costs and timelines. You're prepared to make decisions based on goals, not emotions.

You know how to eat this elephant.

Stop making excuses and take that first bite.

ACKNOWLEDGMENTS

Being a perfectionist, this book—the original and this revision—would have taken me decades to finish were it not for my husband, Walt Hampton, who has the uncanny ability to turn absolutely everything into a friendly competition, including writing and publishing books. For his relentless encouragement, his talent for making me laugh when I take myself too seriously, and his unwavering belief in this project, I thank him.

I'd also like to acknowledge my former partners at East Hill Writers' Workshop, Anne Batterson and Sherry Horton, who taught me more about the craft of writing than I ever learned in any classroom. You can't ask for better friends, mentors, and creative collaborators. Our years together shaped my understanding of what it means to serve writers with integrity and excellence.

To my team at Summit Press Publishers: Thank you for the exceptional work you do in helping create beautiful, highly readable, valuable books that make our authors look like the superstars they truly are. Your dedication to quality and your commitment to our authors' success make everything we do possible.

To the authors who have placed their trust in Summit Press Publishers: Your books aren't just your legacy—they are your business-building tools, your platforms for change, and your gifts to readers who need precisely what you have to offer. Thank you for allowing us to be part of your journey from manuscript to published author. Watching you succeed is the greatest reward of this work.

And finally, to my many students and coaching clients over the years who have poured their hearts onto the page, who have been willing to dig deep and get vulnerable, who have gone back to the drawing board when necessary, who have remained open to feedback even when it stung, and who have created truly remarkable work: I am honored to have been part of your writing journey. Your courage and dedication inspire me every day.

This book exists because of you all. Thank you for teaching me as much as I've hopefully taught you.

ABOUT THE AUTHOR

ANN SHEYBANI is the founder and publisher of Summit Press Publishers, where she transforms business professionals into published authors whose books enhance their credibility and accelerate their success.

After earning her master's degree in writing from Harvard University, Ann founded East Hill Writers' Workshop to serve literary writers. Everything changed when Tony Robbins' coaching colleagues recruited her to teach entrepreneurs how to write books. This pivot revealed what most writing advice misses entirely: books aren't just creative expression—they're strategic business assets.

Today, Ann specializes in helping coaches, consultants, and subject matter experts create professionally polished books that serve dual purposes: delivering genuine value to readers while opening doors for authors. She's guided hundreds of professionals through every stage of the publishing process because she understands that brilliant content without smart strategy is just expensive therapy.

At Summit Press Publishers, Ann and her team maintain an exclusive focus on business professionals who understand that books are investments, not vanity projects. Her authors consistently report that their book investment returns multiples through enhanced credibility, premium client attraction, and new business opportunities.

When she's not helping authors build their strategic publishing plans, Ann enjoys running, traveling, and discovering new ways to help writers work smarter, not harder.

Connect with Ann at ann@summitpresspublishers.com

The Seven Book
Blueprint Templates...and more

Ready to build your own blueprint? These seven detailed templates show you exactly what content you need to create based on the type of book you want to write. Each template is modeled after a successful book in its genre and includes specific questions you must answer for every chapter, helping you determine your logic flow and organizational schema before you start writing. Whether you're planning a research-based authority book (Brené Brown model), a story-driven insight book (Psychology of Money model), a business book with backend offerings (Jeff Walker model), a method-based instruction manual (KonMari model), a modular how-to guide (Michael Port model), a transformation memoir (Educated model), or a blog-to-book collection (Minimalists model), these templates eliminate the guesswork and give you a proven structure to follow. Download your complete template collection (and more) at www.summitpresspublishers.com/brick and start building your book with confidence.